FUN IN
LONDON
1988

FODOR'S TRAVEL PUBLICATIONS
New York & London

ISBN 0–679–01509–4
ISBN 0–340–41963–6 (Hodder and Stoughton)

Maps and plans by Jon Bauch,
Swanston Graphics, and
London Regional Transport
Illustrations by Ted Burwell

New titles in the series

Maui

New Orleans

Rio

Riviera

also available

Acapulco

Bahamas

Las Vegas

Montreal

New York City

Orlando Area

Paris

Puerto Rico

St. Martin/Sint Maarten

San Francisco

Waikiki

MANUFACTURED IN THE UNITED STATES OF AMERICA
10 9 8 7 6 5 4 3 2 1

Contents

General Information

The London tourist season starts on January 1 and ends on December 31. In the peak months of July and August hotels are filled to capacity, restaurant service is strained, and you'll have to wait on line for such top sights as the Crown Jewels. Better to aim for late April, May, and early June, before the heaviest flood of tourists storms the city, or September, after most have headed home again.

The meteorological term for British weather is maritime. Another name could be cussed, or unpredictable. Twice in the past ten years, London has sweltered through long summers, with temperatures touching 90 degrees—air conditioning units and swimming pools sold wildly, only to be left unused the following year as summer brought extremes of grey skies, rain, and what weathermen call "sunny periods." But you don't go to a capital city to get a suntan and lie on a beach. Besides, cooler weather is preferable for sightseeing.

An average summer will be a cocktail of warm sunshine, overcast skies, showers, and fair humidity. Spring is the same, but cooler. Autumn can be pleasant, with warm days sometimes extending into late October. Winter brings unrelenting greyness relieved by occasional sharp blue-sky days, gales, rainstorms, and some snow (the latter rarely lasts for long). Winter temperatures hover around the 40-degree mark.

On the positive side, you can forget those B-movie shots of swirling yellow fog flickering around gas lamps. No longer can Frank Sinatra sing of "a foggy day in London town," thanks to the Clean Air Act, which bans burning smokey fuels in urban areas. Pollution from car fumes is as bad as in any major city, but "pea-soupers," as London's impenetrable smogs were called, are gone forever.

Whatever the season or the weather, no visitor to London will ever have to sit in his hotel room playing Scrabble. With a heritage stretching back many centuries B.C., London has scores of historic sites, museums, and galleries that remain open all year. As a world center for the arts, barely a week passes without a major opening of an exhibition, the first night of a new play or musical, or the performance of a new musical work.

WHAT TO PACK

Take the most comfortable pair of shoes you can buy, a collapsible umbrella, a lightweight raincoat for spring and summer (a warmer coat and scarf for autumn and winter), and sweaters for cool summer nights. All of these could be considered essential when heading to London. On the other hand, should you want to add to your wardrobe you could pack as few clothes as possible and buy more when you arrive according to the prevailing elements (and styles).

To dispel another old Hollywood myth, not all Englishmen wear pin-stripe suits and bowler hats; nor do they necessarily carry rolled up umbrellas—although these are still the accepted "uniform" of more traditional bastions of the City district (City with a capital C referring to the old, walled district most commonly known for the Tower of London).

Jeans, and all the possible designer variations on them, are as ubiquitous here as anywhere else in the world. Smart casual dress is accepted in most hotels, restaurants, theaters, and concert halls. Some hotels, such as the Savoy or the Connaught, still expect a man to wear a jacket and tie when dining, and frown on women in pants suits. Similarly, there is a new breed of nightclub that turns away customers not attired in a manner deemed fashionable—though this may have nothing to do with ties, jackets, or formal gowns.

As a general rule, Londoners like to dress well when going to the West End, the center for nightlife and restaurants—except on rare hot summer nights when the weather dictates informality. Follow their example if it makes you feel more comfortable, but, no matter what the season, you won't be thrown out if you prefer to be more casual.

TRIP TIPS

Most U.S. visitors to London will arrive by air at one of its two airports—Heathrow, 14 miles to the west, or Gatwick, 28 miles to the south. (Luckier travelers will dock at Southampton on the *QE2* or a similar liner, and should take the train to Waterloo station in the center of the city.) Both airports can be appallingly congested and you can expect long waits as you clear immigration and customs during peak summer months.

Heathrow is the busier of the two, but has the best access to London—by Underground, the British subway system also known as the tube—from two stations beneath the airport, one serving terminals 1 through 3, the other the recently built terminal 4. The trip takes about 40 minutes and costs £1.60; the train links directly with the central London system, so you can transfer to whatever line takes you closest to your hotel or other destination. There is also a frequent Airbus service from

Heathrow to the major central London hotels. It costs £3 (dollars accepted). London's "black cab" taxis wait outside the Heathrow terminal. A journey to Hyde Park Corner should cost about £17 on the meter. Make sure the meter is running; pay only that amount, plus tip. As anywhere, there are some cabbies waiting to prey on unsuspecting tourists by offering them an off-meter "special" rate.

The best way to travel from Gatwick into London is by British Rail from the station within the airport. This service was modernized in 1984 with new, high-speed, air-conditioned trains making the 30-minute journey every 15 minutes. The trains are also used by ordinary commuters, but airline passengers and their baggage have special facilities. The trains take you to Victoria Station in the Westminster district of central London. If you want to travel on by tube to a station nearer your hotel, you can buy a combined rail/tube ticket at the Gatwick station. The route from Gatwick to London by car is first on highway then through dreary suburbs. Take the train. It costs £4.60.

Don't even think of renting a car at either airport if you plan to stay in London. Parking lots are expensive and few and far between. It is unlikely that your hotel will have a garage, and on-street parking is very difficult and hazardous. Illegal cars are fined and clamped. If you want a car to explore other parts of England once you leave London, then rent it on the day you leave. All the usual rental firms have offices in most cities. But—be warned that British gasoline is heavily taxed. An Imperial gallon (a bit more than its U.S. counterpart) is around £1.80.

MONEY

The airport banks will be open whatever time you arrive, but there are usually long lines and the rates aren't advantageous, so change some dollars to pounds before you leave the U.S. London's banks are open weekdays from 9:30 A.M. to 3:30 P.M. (except Barclays and National

Westminster, which open some of their branches Saturday mornings). Central London is well served with *bureau de change* kiosks. Some may give better rates than the banks, but as they charge a percentage, any benefit is usually wiped out. It pays to shop around. It will usually be more expensive to change money at hotels, restaurants, and stores than at banks.

Travelers checks are acceptable as payment in most shops, restaurants, and hotels, and some shops offer discounts for payment this way. You'll find credit cards also widely accepted, but some establishments don't take all of them, and a few shops and restaurants won't take any—check the doors and windows for the usual stickers. American Express and Diners Club look the same in the U.K. as they do in the U.S., but Visa is also known as Barclaycard, and Mastercard is also known as Access.

TIME

The U.K. is five hours ahead of U.S. Eastern Standard Time, on Greenwich Mean Time in winter and European Summer Time from March through October.

ENTRY AND CUSTOMS

U.S. citizens must have a passport prior to arrival; a visitor's visa is issued upon entering the country. Immigration and customs forms are distributed on planes and ships prior to arrival. No vaccinations are needed.

The first $400 of merchandise purchased per person in the same family is duty free upon returning home. Before your trip, register any merchandise made in the U.K. but bought in the U.S. at the Customs office at your airport in the United States.

If you're the kind of traveler who *has* to take your pet boa constrictor along, be warned that there's a very strict surveillance at British Customs to prevent the entry of all animals. Fines and penalties are rigidly enforced, and woe betide anyone who tries a spot of pet smuggling.

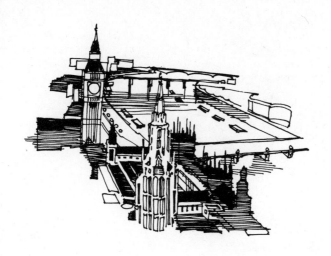

Introduction

It is some 200 years since that English man of letters, Dr. Samuel Johnson, was moved to write: "When a man is tired of London he is tired of life, for there is in London all that life can afford."

The London of the latter half of the 20th century is somewhat different than that of Dr. Johnson's day, but no Madison Avenue copywriter could better his description of this teeming capital city and all that it has to offer.

One of London's greatest assets—especially for the visitor who prefers the role of traveler to tourist—is that apart from its familiar historical sights and wide-ranging amenities, it is also very much a living city with a vast residential population and an almost constantly advancing and retreating army of commuters.

Escalating property prices and planners' efforts to decentralize mean that many houses in the center of London that used to be homes are now offices or shops. But newly enlightened urban policies—and the drudgery of commuting—are serving to stabilize the population. New homes are being created right in the heart of London, most notably in the revitalized Covent Garden area—though at greatly inflated prices.

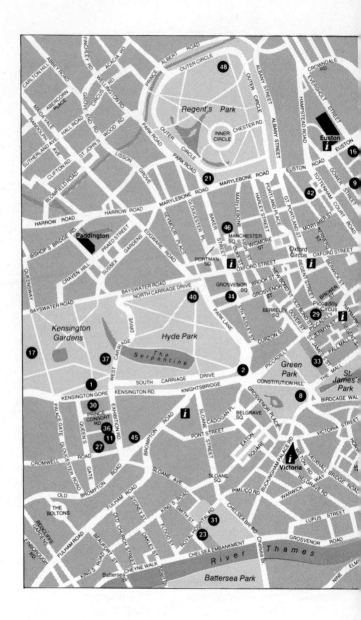

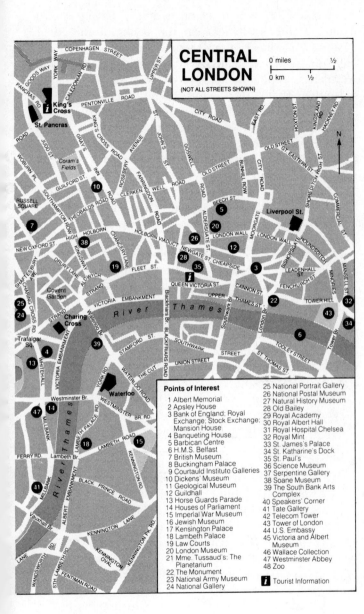

CENTRAL LONDON

(NOT ALL STREETS SHOWN)

0 miles   ½
0 km   ½

Points of Interest

1 Albert Memorial
2 Apsley House
3 Bank of England; Royal
  Exchange; Stock Exchange;
  Mansion House
4 Banqueting House
5 Barbican Centre
6 H.M.S. Belfast
7 British Museum
8 Buckingham Palace
9 Courtauld Institute Galleries
10 Dickens' Museum
11 Geological Museum
12 Guildhall
13 Horse Guards Parade
14 Houses of Parliament
15 Imperial War Museum
16 Jewish Museum
17 Kensington Palace
18 Lambeth Palace
19 Law Courts
20 London Museum
21 Mme. Tussaud's; The
   Planetarium
22 The Monument
23 National Army Museum
24 National Gallery
25 National Portrait Gallery
26 National Postal Museum
27 Natural History Museum
28 Old Bailey
29 Royal Academy
30 Royal Albert Hall
31 Royal Hospital Chelsea
32 Royal Mint
33 St. James's Palace
34 St. Katharine's Dock
35 St. Paul's
36 Science Museum
37 Serpentine Gallery
38 Soane Museum
39 The South Bank Arts
   Complex
40 Speakers' Corner
41 Tate Gallery
42 Telecom Tower
43 Tower of London
44 U.S. Embassy
45 Victoria and Albert
   Museum
46 Wallace Collection
47 Westminster Abbey
48 Zoo

i Tourist Information

Greater London is 34 miles across, having grown from a Celtic settlement on the banks of the River Thames some five centuries B.C. Despite waves of invading armies—the Romans, Vikings, Saxons, Danes, and Normans; despite the plague of 1665 that wiped out more than 75,000 inhabitants; despite the Great Fire of 1666 that raged through and destroyed four-fifths of the old City of London; and despite the bombings of World War II, London has expanded to its present sprawling proportions, engulfing villages and fields in the development of suburban areas.

Luckily for the visitor, much of London's historic, artistic, and/or hedonistic treasures are contained within a relatively small area, easily accessible via short trips on public transportation, or, better yet, on foot.

They are concentrated into three main areas:

- The City, site of an original Roman encampment and occupying a square mile north of Tower Bridge. Containing many fascinating legacies of its ancestors, this is now London's financial/business district. Note that it is this area that Londoners refer to when they talk of "the City," and not London as a whole.

- The central area, including the West End (west of the City, that is) from Marylebone in the north, to the Embankment in the south, and west to Knightsbridge. These districts are home to most shops, nightlife, restaurants, and hotels, plus Buckingham Palace and Westminster.

- The Knightsbridge/Kensington/Chelsea sections of West London—partly residential, partly smart shops, museums, parks, and hotels.

With the notable exception of the South Bank arts center on the other side of the Thames, the sites of 16th-century and Elizabethan theaters including Shakespeare's Globe, and the Imperial War Museum, there is little in South London to interest visitors. North London's principal attractions are Hampstead Heath, with its rolling parkland on a hill high above the city, now a fashionable residential district; and the street markets at Camden Passage and Camden Lock.

Coming to terms with London needs a little thought and planning, but there is no better way to establish bearings than by taking one of the frequent sightseeing bus tours.

London Regional Transport (222–1234) runs tours using its bright double-decker buses every half hour between 10 A.M. and 5 P.M. from Victoria (Grosvenor Gardens), Marble Arch and Piccadilly Circus. If you buy a ticket at the Travel Centers at either Piccadilly underground station or Victoria Station it costs £4.50, £2.50 for those under 16; on the bus it costs 50p extra. During the summer an hour-long night tour costs £2 and £1, respectively.

Other tours operated by independent firms offer varying degrees of comfort, expertise in particular areas (art or history, for example), or include meals and entertainment. The most luxurious of all? Take the bus decked out in the distinctive green and gold livery of the internationally renowned Harrods department store—complete with refreshments and commentary in eight languages. Three times a day, year round. £12 for adults and £7.50 for children.

The sights that you will want to return to will include Buckingham Palace (home of the Queen); the Houses of Parliament and Westminster Abbey; the Tower of London; the British Museum; Trafalgar Square and the National Gallery; St. Paul's and the City; Covent Garden; Piccadilly and the theater district; the Royal Albert Hall and the Albert Memorial; the South Bank arts center; the Kensington museums and parks; and the River Thames, itself offering a variety of outings.

Many of London's finest attractions are available entirely free for the visitor who is prepared to use his or her feet and eyes. London's 2,000-year history is reflected in its architecture—Roman remains in the City, Gothic and Wren churches, elegant Georgian and Regency crescents and squares, leafy Victorian terraces, and the modern designs of the National Theatre and Barbican.

The amount of green parkland remaining protected in central London often surprises visitors. The best perspective is from the restaurant at the top of the Hilton Hotel (22 Park Lane; 493–8000). From here you look down on Hyde Park as it stretches to Kensington Gardens. These are both Royal Parks—so designated because they were at one time private land owned by one or another of Britain's many sovereigns. Though still owned by today's Royal Family, they are open to all.

As befits a city that was once the trading capital of the biggest Empire in the world, London's shopping facilities are unsurpassed. Oxford Street, long and straight, running from Marble Arch to Tottenham Court Road, is the main shopping artery. But it is best avoided (especially on Saturdays) except for forays to the big department stores, and those are best made first thing in the morning, before the crowds swarm out.

Old Bond Street and New Bond Street (invariably lumped together as Bond Street) combine to make London's smartest shopping avenue. Bisecting Mayfair from Oxford Street to Piccadilly, Bond Street (nobody uses the "Old" and "New" very much) has some of the city's top fashion and jewelry shops, as do Regent Street and Knightsbridge.

Younger fashion shops are on South Molton Street in Mayfair and King's Road in Chelsea; antique shops can be found along Kensington Church Street, New King's Road, Bond Street, and Knightsbridge; books are the main merchandise on Charing Cross Road and the surrounding narrow lanes; Covent Garden and its area are bursting with smart boutiques and intriguing specialty shops; Jermyn Street is for men's shirts and shoes; Tottenham Court Road is noted for hi-fi, video and computer equipment.

Art and sculpture from prehistoric times to modern day are contained in the British Museum, the Victoria and Albert Museum, and the National and Tate galleries. Two additions are the long-awaited Theater Museum in Covent Garden, and the Clore Gallery—an extension to the Tate Gallery—devoted to the works of Turner. Check for special exhibitions at the Royal Academy, the Hayward Gallery, and the Barbican, as well as at the commercial galleries around Bond Street.

London's literary heritage is waiting to be discovered in almost every street, but perhaps most of all in the Bloomsbury district adjacent to the British Museum. Here such writers, artists, and critics as Virginia Woolf, Roger Fry, D. H. Lawrence, and Rupert Brooke made their home. The area also contains London's University College; the quiet 19th-century squares here take on a campus atmosphere when school is in session.

London has more theaters and concert halls and a wider range of performing arts entertainment than most cities in the world. There will never be any problem in finding something to suit your taste. London's theaters are also generally well preserved, with plush red seats, ornate gilt decorations, and original wood-and-plaster paneling. They are worth visiting for the sense of occasion as well as for whatever might be happening on stage.

There is almost always an opera or ballet playing at the Royal Opera House, the Coliseum, or Sadler's Wells. The Royal Shakespeare Company performs at the Barbican, and the Festival Hall and Royal Albert Hall have regular classical concerts. Other forms of nightlife include the usual "international" nightclubs with a floorshow and cabaret (though nothing on the scale of Las Vegas), plus a wide selection of discos and several fine jazz venues.

Eating out presents a special problem: an overabundance of choices. A culinary revolution has transformed British eating habits; ironically, it is still difficult to get a good *English* meal, yet the range of food available in London's restaurants is as cosmopolitan as you could wish.

Most hotels provide a Continental breakfast of rolls, jam, and beverages, or a traditional English breakfast of eggs and bacon, and serve tea from 4 P.M. to 6 P.M. Restaurants serve lunch from 12:30 to 3 P.M. (though a law extending licensing hours when accompanying a meal could change this); dinner can be any time between 6:30 and 11 P.M. (As will be noted in the restaurant chapter, there are a number of establishments open later.) Also, there are brasseries, cafés, and fast-food chains of varying quality that provide hot food throughout the day.

Snacks can be found in most of London's several thousand pubs. They are in themselves a unique part of English life and should be included on your list of things to see and do. The word pub is a widely used diminutive for public house, a place to have a drink and meet your friends, usually a much more traditional watering hole than the normal American bar.

Throughout London you will come across wine bars, a cross between a restaurant and pub where, as the name suggests, you can sit and drink a glass or bottle of wine, with or without a modest meal. Non-liquid refreshments usually include quiche or casseroles or simply cheese and crackers.

After all that sightseeing, theater-going, culture, and gourmandizing, you may wish to escape from London for a few hours or more. Take a leisurely trip along the Thames to Greenwich or Richmond; or venture further out of town to Stratford-on-Avon (birthplace of William Shakespeare); the University town of Oxford; the cathedral town of Canterbury; or the seaside resort of Brighton, with its Regency Pavilion. All these—and many more—are perfectly possible as day trips, either by rail, by car, or on one of the many organized tours that are on offer.

Getting Around

The best way to see London is to walk its streets, squares, and parks. However, given its sprawling layout, there will be occasions when you will need to resort to public transportation or taxis. One immediate word of warning: Avoid the underground subway—or the tube as Londoners call it—during the rush hours, 7:30 to 9 A.M. and 4:45 to 6:30 P.M.

London's Underground system is a vast network of nine lines criss-crossing the city in various directions. It is also the most efficient means of transportation for all but very short distances. For longer rides, buses will of course provide a view, but the tube will almost always be faster.

Anyone who has used New York's blighted subway should be reassured that London's Underground is relatively civilized and safe (though mugging, sadly, is a growing problem on certain lines, and at some central stations in particular). At least, the graffiti are limited to moustaches drawn on posters, or the odd slogan. Alas, pickpockets, too, abound, so watch your purse or wallet.

Getting about on the tube is not too difficult once you have mastered the color codes, the names of the lines, and the interchange system, which are less confusing than they sound. Pick up a full-color pocket map at any station and you will soon be able to work out your plan; for instance, to travel from Knightsbridge to St. Paul's, you take the dark blue Piccadilly Line going north and change at Holborn onto the red Central Line going east. There are large-scale maps at all stations, at interchanges, and on all platforms indicating the direction in which that train goes.

If you are to be in London for a few days and intend to use the tube and buses regularly, LRT has several bargain cards available, among them the One Week Travelcard, which provides travel on both bus and tube, *in* as well as *out of* the rush hour; price depends on the number of zones you plan to cover. For two zones, including Central, you'll pay £6; for all five, £14.30. As we write, LRT is planning a replacement for the London Explorer Pass—phone 222-1234 for details.

If you prefer to purchase individual tickets as you go, you will be able to do so at numerous slot-machine ticket dispensers located at the entrance to every station or at manned booths. The basic fare is 50p for travel within a single zone (70p for two zones) no matter how many times you change lines. There are signs above the slot machines indicating fares to stations, arranged in alphabetical order. If in doubt, just ask.

Most stations have automatic ticket barriers that open when you push your ticket into a slot at the front—but remember to retrieve your ticket when it pops out the slot on top; a ticket collector will take it from you when you reach your final destination.

London Regional Transport bans cigarette smoking on all tubes and below-ground station tracks. Last trains usually leave central London between midnight and 1 A.M., earlier on Sundays. London Transport travel information is available 24 hours by calling 222–1234.

London's bus network is even more comprehensive than the underground; a map of it is included on the tube

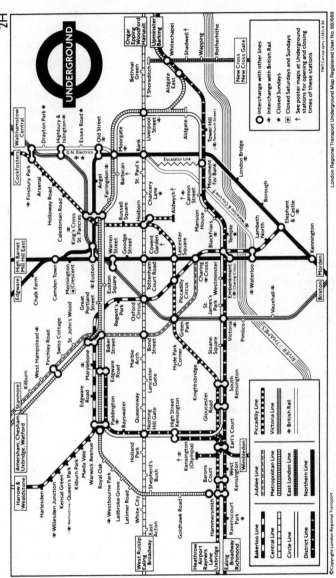

map. Some bus stops have the word "request" on them, which means you have to raise your hand to stop an approaching bus. Most buses have conductors, but on some you pay the driver upon boarding. Fares are again based on zones—tell the conductor your destination and he'll tell you the fare (unless you have a pass).

Londoners—with some unruly exceptions—expect you to line up (they call it queuing) in an orderly fashion at the stops, each of which has a map indicating the routes of the buses along that street. There is limited all-night service on some routes.

The other alternative for getting around is to take one of London's famous "black cabs," expensive as they may be. In fact, they are not all black nowadays. They can come in a variety of colors, but are still among the most sensible and comfortable public vehicles anywhere. A typical hop downtown will run £2 or £3. If you hail a cab with its yellow "For Hire" sign illuminated, the driver is bound by law to take you to your destination within a six-mile radius (or to Heathrow). If you want to go further the fare is subject to negotiation. Tip about 20p on fares up to £1.50 and ten percent above that.

Once upon a time, London's cabbies were salt-of-the-earth characters, always ready to leap out and help you with luggage, and anxious to discuss the latest political scandal or their rheumatism. Sadly, today's appalling traffic conditions have changed all that. But the black cab drivers' knowledge of London's myriad streets is still legendary. You can telephone for a black cab at 263-9496.

The City

The City of London, as the square mile commencing at the world famous Tower of London is known, is the true historical center of what is today Greater London. It is the site of the most popular tourist attractions—the aforementioned Tower of London, Tower Bridge, and St. Paul's Cathedral—and also an area of fascinating Dickensian side streets and ancient pubs, churches, and buildings. There is only one way to explore the City, and that is by allowing plenty of time to wander its streets, detouring down side alleys, popping into its churches, and visiting its historic buildings.

The City is also the commercial center of London and as such there are just as many plain, boring buildings and streets as interesting ones. The restaurants here cater mainly to business executives and office workers, so this isn't an area for a relaxing meal, though the numerous pubs will usually provide a substantial snack or a light repast along with your pint of beer. Certainly, you should not choose to eat in the City at night, as most restaurants are closed.

Several yards beneath your feet in the City are the

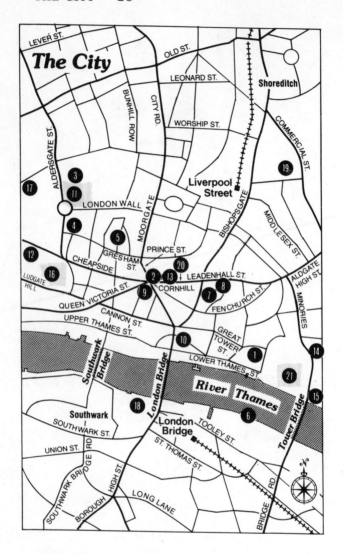

Points of Interest

1 All Hallows by the Tower Church
2 Bank of England
3 Barbican Arts Center
4 Church of St. Anne & St. Agnes
5 Guildhall
6 HMS Belfast
7 Leadenhall Market
8 Lloyd's
9 Mansion House
10 Monument
11 Museum of London

12 Old Bailey
13 Royal Exchange
14 Royal Mint
15 St. Katharine's Dock
16 St. Paul's Cathedral
17 Smithfield Market
18 Southwark Cathedral
19 Spitalfield Market
20 Stock Exchange
21 Tower of London

sidewalks of Londinium, the encampment established by the invading Roman army in A.D. 43.

At the beginning of the third century A.D., a wall two yards high and more than a mile long was built around Londinium, with gateways for the roads leading out of town. Remains of the wall, rebuilt over the centuries, still stand.

In 1984, a well-marked self-guiding tour along the route of the Roman walls and defenses was inaugurated by the Museum of London (Barbican, London Wall; 600–3699). The two-hour walk starts just north of the Tower of London and ends at the museum. A descriptive map and guide can be obtained from the museum; it also contains many relics of ancient and Modern London—from a Roman writing tablet to a Woolworth's counter and its array of goods. Open Tuesday to Saturday 10 A.M. to 6 P.M., Sunday 2 to 6 P.M.; free.

An ideal way of covering most of the City's key sights would be to take the Wall Walk in reverse, getting a feel of the history of the place from the Museum first, then walking to the Tower, where you should allow at least two hours for sightseeing. (If you prefer to go straight to the Tower, take the tube on the Circle or District lines to Tower Hill station.) Then tour the rest of the City, as detailed later in this chapter.

The Tower of London is one of London's most-visited tourist attractions. Its central keep—the White Tower—was built for William the Conqueror the year after his 1066 invasion as a vantage point down river and as a deterrent to rebellious conquered Britons.

Succeeding sovereigns enhanced its defenses and fortifications, by including towers and moats, a barracks and a royal residence. Throughout history it served as a formidable prison, its inmates including Richard II, Henry VI, the Little Princes, Anne Boleyn, Sir Walter Raleigh, and Guy Fawkes (who plotted to blow up Parliament). The last person to be imprisoned there was Rudolph Hess in 1941.

Executions were carried out—and victims buried—on what is now Tower Green, inside the walls. There was a scaffold for public hangings outside on Tower Hill;

some were beheaded with an ax and the heads displayed on spikes to deter others.

On a happier note, the Jewel House in the Tower contains the priceless and glorious Crown Jewels, which includes St. Edward's crown, made for Charles II and last worn by the present Queen at her 1953 coronation.

Look out for the "Beefeaters"—symbol of London on many a postcard—the Tower Yeoman Warders in their traditional Tudor dress. Also spot the famous black ravens strutting the lawns. Legend has it that the Sovereign will fall should the ravens leave.

The Tower of London (709–0765) is open from 9:30 A.M. to 5 P.M. Monday through Saturday; 2 to 5 P.M. Sunday from March to October; and from 9:30 A.M. to 4 P.M. November to February, Monday to Saturday only. Entrance fee: £4 (£2 for under 16s).

Nearby, straddling the Thames, stands Tower Bridge (407–0922), the last bridge over the river before the estuary. It is relatively modern, having been completed in 1894, though it was designed to blend in with the Tower. It is a three-span steel bridge with a two-leaf drawbridge.

The walkway along the steel-girded permanent bridge linking the top of the twin towers is open to the public and provides a magnificent viewpoint up and down the Thames and across to the Tower. There is also an exhibition room and a film show, museum, and shop. It is open 10 A.M. to 6:30 P.M., April to October, and 10 A.M. to 4:45 P.M., November to March (£2, children £1).

Retrace your steps to the Tower and turn right for a relaxing stroll—and maybe some refreshment—around St. Katharine's Dock, a new marina on the site of a working dock dating back to 1827. In its heyday, the dock became a treasure trove as ships unloaded ivory, silver, and valuable spices from all over the world. But as ships became larger, docks further down river took over. World War II bombing finally put an end to the dock's working life.

In the 1960s work began on breathing new life into London's docklands. The old warehouses around St. Katharine's Dock have been turned into apartments, a yachting clubhouse, bars, and restaurants. Nearby are the newly-built World Trade Centre and Tower Hotel.

Have a drink of "real ale" at the **Dickens Inn** (St. Katharine's Way; 488–1226), itself a restoration of a late 1700 warehouse. The building also houses the Pickwick Room restaurant with English dishes such as steak and kidney pie and the Dickens Room specializing in fish dishes.

To walk through the City, return to Tower Hill tube station and cross Trinity Square and its garden into Byward Street. The church on the left—All Hallows-by-the-Tower—has a 17th-century square brick tower, which diarist Samuel Pepys climbed in 1666 to view the desolation after the Great Fire. William Penn, founder of Pennsylvania, was baptized here.

Bear right onto Great Tower Street and Eastcheap and you'll soon glimpse the top of The Monument, a fluted column 202 feet high, built in 1667 to commemorate the Great Fire. It is on Fish Street Hill, but to reach it turn left down Pudding Lane, where the fire was reputed to have started. If you fancy climbing to the top, be warned that there are 311 steps, and the view isn't that great once you get there. It is open 9 A.M. to 4 P.M. Monday through Saturday, and 2 to 6 P.M. on Sunday in summer. Entrance: 50p, children 25p.

Walk back up Gracechurch Street. The modern skyscraper tower ahead is the head office of the National Westminster Bank, contrasting with the church of St. Peter-upon-Cornhill on your right, which stands on the site of the oldest church in the City (A.D. 179). On the right, spend some time exploring the Leadenhall Market, with its meat, fish, and game shops, and maybe take a drink at the New Moon pub on Gracechurch Street. There has been a market on this site since Roman times, but the present building dates from the 1800s. In Lime Street, look in at the new Lloyd's of London building

(623–7100) designed by the architect of Paris's Pompidou Center, Richard Rogers. Then turn left into Threadneedle Street, passing the Stock Exchange on the right, the Royal Exchange on the left (where trading began in the 17th century), and the Bank of England farther ahead on the right. The latter faces the magnificent Mansion House, official residence of the Lord Mayor of London.

Follow Princes Street alongside the Bank of England and turn left onto Gresham Street. On the right is the Guildhall, headquarters of the Corporation of London, which governs the City. Some of its walls and crypt are as they were in the 15th century. Visit the Great Hall (Monday to Saturday 10 A.M. to 5 P.M.), the Guildhall Library (Monday to Saturday 9:30 A.M. to 5 P.M.) and the Clock Museum (Monday to Friday 9:30 A.M. to 4:45 P.M.)

The Baron of Beef, Gutter Lane (606–6961) is one of the few City restaurants with a welcoming atmosphere for tourists. This is the perfect place to try the British specialty of roast beef (served from a trolley) with roast potatoes and Yorkshire pudding. In a large basement, the restaurant is decorated in baronial style with a fleur-de-lys ceiling and walls paneled with oak. The service is equally old-fashioned. Lunch for two will cost around £35. Closed Sat. and Sun.

Nearby Gresham Street has an interesting church, St. Anne and St. Agnes, originally built around 1200. It was rebuilt by Sir Christopher Wren after the Great Fire, then again after the war using Wren's original red-brick design. It is now a Lutheran church with services in Estonian and Latvian, as well as in English.

Turn right along Aldersgate Street if you wish to return to the Museum of London and/or visit the Barbican arts center behind it—part of an experiment in new urban planning with towering apartment buildings, raised walkways, gardens, and fountains.

To see more of the City, turn left along St. Martin's Le Grand and head for the magnificent dome of Wren's St. Paul's Cathedral. The dome majestically dominates the ugly modern office buildings that surround it.

Any Londoner who lived through World War II has a soft spot for St. Paul's. It miraculously survived the bombs that rained around it then. But the 13th-century church, which was devastated by the Great Fire in 1666, was already the third or fourth church on the site. The present Wren-designed cathedral took 33 years to build. During this time Wren drew plans for 51 other City churches.

Your visit to St. Paul's should include the inside of the dome and the "whispering gallery," so-called because the acoustics are said to transmit even a whisper. See also the High Altar of marble and carved oak, the crypt with the tombs of Sir Christopher Wren, Lord Nelson, and the Duke of Wellington, and memorials to many other famous men and women from Britain's past. You may also attend services and concerts in the Cathedral. Check for details by calling 248-2705, or the City Information Center (606-3030) opposite the Cathedral.

Down Ludgate Hill, and off to the right, is Old Bailey, the street that lends its name to the Central Criminal Court. It stands on the site of courts and prisons going back to the Middle Ages. In 1670, William Penn, the English Quaker who went on to found Pennsylvania, was tried here for "preaching to an unlawful assembly." Ironically, the *jury* was jailed and fined for returning a verdict of not guilty!

Today, the gold figure of a lady holding scales and sword in outstretched arms that crowns the building is synonymous with British justice and has been featured in many a grade-B movie. Opposite are two typical City pubs: The George (25 Old Bailey; 248–5609) where you can join in a game of darts, or partake of homemade steak and kidney pie; and The Magpie & Stump (18 Old Bailey; 248–3819), which was a favorite meeting place to watch public executions in the notorious Newgate Prison that stood opposite it in the late 18th century.

Le Gamin, 32 Old Bailey (236–7931), is a light and airy basement French restaurant owned by the Roux brothers, who have an international reputation for running fine restaurants, including Le Gavroche (Mayfair) and Waterside Inn (Bray, Berkshire). This one has a good-value set menu that includes a kir, radish dips, wine, coffee, and petit fours. Main courses can include steak in red wine or lamb in herbs, and there are good desserts and French cheeses. Open only for lunch and you must have reservations. Expect to pay not less than £30 for two.

Continuing down Ludgate Hill brings you to Fleet Street, world famous for its newspaper offices and, in a narrow alley off to the left, Gough Square. Here, at No. 17, Dr. Samuel Johnson lived from 1748 to 1759, compiling his dictionary. (Open 10:30 A.M. to 5 P.M. Monday to Saturday.) After visiting, follow in Dr. Johnson's footsteps to the nearby hostelry, Ye Old Cheshire Cheese in Wine Office Court (353–6170), which is well preserved since being rebuilt in 1667. It has three restaurants in all—including a Chop House serving traditional English staples—as well as three bars.

Further along Fleet Street, off to the left, is The Temple—not a religious building, but an area of quiet houses and gardens, for many centuries the site of the homes and offices of solicitors barristers whose work now takes them to the Law Courts at the top of Fleet Street. The impressive building was designed by Barry, architect of the House of Parliament.

Here the City ends and the rest of London begins.

Covent Garden and Bloomsbury

Covent Garden's garden, part of a monastery, disappeared in the 16th century, but the name has remained. Today it is the site of an astonishingly successful center-city redevelopment.

Former 19th-century fruit and vegetable market buildings have been transformed into attractive shops, bars, and restaurants; old warehouses have become dance studios, rehearsal rooms, and photographic studios; and street musicians and players provide free open-air entertainment. Unusually for London, it's all going seven days a week and even the shops stay open until late. Open-air cafés create a very un-English, Continental atmosphere.

Bounded by the Strand, Charing Cross Road, Shaftesbury Avenue, and Drury Lane, Covent Garden's center is its Italian-style piazza, designed by the King's surveyor, Inigo Jones, in the 17th century. A market has existed on the site for 300 years, while two ornate Central Market buildings were added in 1830. The latter helped

Points of Interest

1 Admiralty Arch
2 British Museum
3 Buckingham Palace
4 Burlington Arcade
5 Cabinet War Rooms
6 Carlton House
7 Cenotaph
8 Clarence House
9 Covent Garden Market/
  Theater Museum
10 Drury Lane Theater
11 Freemasons Hall
12 Horse Guards
   Parade
13 Houses of
   Parliament
14 John Nash's Church
   of All Souls
15 Lancaster House
16 Liberty
17 London Coliseum
18 Museum of Mankind
19 National Gallery
20 National Portrait
   Gallery
21 No. 10 Downing
   Street
22 Queen Victoria
   Memorial
23 Royal Academy
24 Royal Opera House
25 St. James's Palace
26 Soane Museum
27 South Bank Arts
   Complex
28 Westminster Abbey

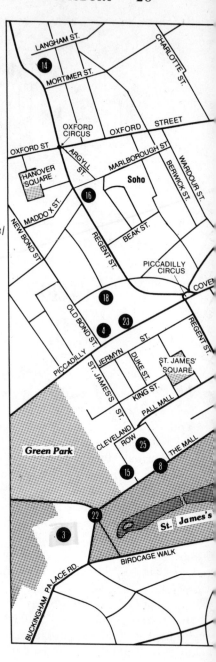

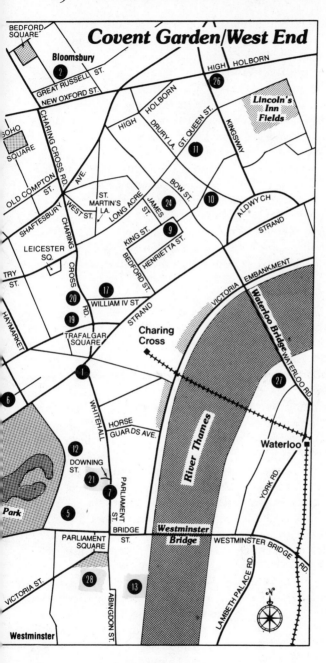

Covent Garden/West End

BEDFORD
SQUARE

Bloomsbury
2

GREAT RUSSELL ST.
NEW OXFORD ST.

HIGH HOLBORN
26

HIGH
HOLBORN

Lincoln's
Inn
Fields

SOHO
SQUARE

CHARING CROSS RD.

OLD COMPTON ST.

DRURY LA.

GT. QUEEN ST.

KINGSWAY

11

ST.
MARTIN'S
LA.

WEST ST.

SHAFTESBURY

LONG ACRE

JAMES ST.

BOW ST.

24

10

ALDWYCH

STRAND

LEICESTER
SQ.

KING ST.

9

HENRIETTA ST.

BEDFORD ST.

CHARING CROSS RD.

TRY
ST.

20

17

WILLIAM IV ST.

STRAND

EMBANKMENT

VICTORIA

Waterloo Bridge

WATERLOO RD.

19

TRAFALGAR
SQUARE

Charing
Cross

HAYMARKET

1

6

27

WHITEHALL

HORSE
GUARDS AVE.

River Thames

Waterloo

12

DOWNING
ST.

21

7

PARLIAMENT ST.

YORK RD.

Park

5

BRIDGE
ST.

Westminster
Bridge

WESTMINSTER BRIDGE RD.

PARLIAMENT
SQUARE

28

13

VICTORIA ST.

ABINGDON ST.

LAMBETH PALACE RD.

N

Westminster

make this London's main fruit, vegetable, and flower market, but also encroached on the surrounding warehouses and workers' cafés and pubs.

By the 1960s, the market caused chaos in the streets as merchants' trucks blocked the narrow approach streets. In 1974, the whole market moved to a new site in south London. Then a battle began between planners and preservationists over the future of the old Covent Garden market buildings.

Eventually, plans to raze the entire area and build new office buildings and a conference center were thrown out and work began on refurbishing the old buildings. The piazza was relaid with cobblestones and banned to traffic. Through the planners' extraordinary ingenuity, the new Covent Garden was able to lure a variety of shops, restaurants, small businesses, and studios.

Avoid the temptation to start a visit to Covent Garden by taking the tube to Covent Garden station—it is desperately overcrowded and even though new elevators are being built, it is best to start your tour from Leicester Square tube (Piccadilly and Northern lines) and walk up Cranbourn Street into Long Acre, passing Stanfords at No. 12–14 (a cornucopia of travel books, guides, and maps), and Bertram Rota at No. 30 for secondhand and antiquarian books.

As you look ahead up Long Acre, the large white building in front of you is the Freemasons Hall, headquarters of the Royal Masonic Institution. Leading off to the left, opposite the tube station, is Neal Street where almost every old building is a new shop.

Back on Long Acre, turn right at James Street; the piazza, with its market buildings, is straight ahead. On the left is the extension to the Royal Opera House, neatly stitched on to the original 1858 building, which has its front on Bow Street. The boutique-style shops on the right were once all market wholesale shops and warehouses, and The White Lion and the Nag's Head pubs, on two corners of Floral Street, are typical former market workers' pubs, seemingly doomed when the market moved away. The have found a new lease of life, and are now thriving concerns catering to the hordes of visitors and office workers who populate the district. Take a drink at one or the other in the evening and you'll find yourself in the company of black-tied musicians from the Opera House, popping out for "a quick one" during the intermission.

Covent Garden Pasta Bar, 30 Henrietta Street (836-8396), is a busy, informally run, two-floor Italian pasta restaurant (no booking). The pasta comes in nine types—all fresh—with a choice of different sauces. A small range of Italian starters, a help-yourself salad bar, and fresh gateaux or sorbet complete the menu. No minimum charge, but a meal averages £5–£8.

The Garden, 29 Maiden Lane (379-0059), is the appropriate name of this family-run wine bar. While they offer exceedingly inexpensive and well chosen wines, the joy of the place is the wholesome home cooking. Enjoy a homemade soup of the day, pork-and-apple pie with cider, or chicken provencal for around £4 a portion.

Tuttons, 11–12 Russell Street (836–1167), is in a prime location, and at the first hint of sunlight tables are laid out on the piazza. The international menu is essentially French with plenty of snacky one-course dishes such as large salads, smoked mackerel mousse, patés and cheese. Main course dishes include baked red mullet, poussin with honey and almonds, plat du jour and plain steak and chops. Minimum charge £4; open till 11.30 P.M. daily.

Inigo Jones, 14 Garrick Street (836–6456). One of the best gourmet bargains in London is served at lunch and between 5:30 and 7 P.M. at this stylish though somewhat austere restaurant. Chef Paul Gayler trained under Anton Mosimann of the Dorchester and his food is light, interesting and in the nouvelle style. £14.75 is the price of this three course meal of outstanding style; expect dishes such as chilled herb soup served with marinaded sliced scallops or mousseline of fresh snails baked in cabbage with hazelnut sauce to start; breast of duckling with a red wine and cinnamon sauce garnished with fresh figs or sliced veal sweetbreads and kidneys baked in pastry with Dublin prawns to follow. To conclude there is cheese (from the revered Pierre Androuet in Paris) or a sweet of the day. Choosing à la carte will put a meal here in the £30-a-head price bracket; wine prices start in earnest at £20 with little under £10. A fine French wine list, with numerous half bottles as well. A vegetarian menu is also available. Closed Sat. lunch and Sun.

The church on the west of the piazza is St. Paul's, popularly known as "the actor's church" because of the stage personalities associated with it. It was designed by Inigo Jones and, in 1795, rebuilt after a fire to his original design. Open Monday to Friday 9:30 A.M. to 4:30 P.M. The Tuscan portico facing the square is featured in the opening scene of George Bernard Shaw's *Pygmalion* and in the stage and film versions of *My Fair Lady*. The first Punch & Judy show—the British children's puppet theater—is reputed to have been seen here in 1662.

The exterior church wall now provides a natural backdrop for the modern-day buskers—musicians and others who perform and then pass the hat as their livelihood.

Wander through the old Covent Garden market buildings and you can explore new shops whose products range from herbs and spices to books, fashions, groceries, chocolates, kitchenware, rare newspapers, film and theater records, and, of course, flowers and vegetables—the latter rather more decorously purveyed than in the days of the original market. Go to **Culpeper** (8) for herbal soaps and lotions, and **Whistles** (20) for mid-price range designer clothes. For the really unusual, look in at **The Doll's House** (29) and, for models and reproductions of toy theaters from Regency, Victorian, and Edwardian times, **Pollock's Toy Theater** (44). Forty original wrought-iron trading stands from the old flower market have also been renovated and are used as stalls for a crafts flea market between the arcades of the shops.

Eating places in the central market provide better-than-average food compared to most tourist centers. It's fun to sit outside the **Bar Crêperie** (36 varieties of crêpes for meals or desserts) watching the buskers and the flow of fellow tourists and office workers. Or you can burrow into the maze of cellars of **The Crusting Pipe** wine bar (Lower Piazza) for a piece of game pie so traditional that they warn you of "lead shot hazard," followed by one of several varieties of vintage port and a piece of strong Stilton cheese.

The nearby Jubilee Market, to the south of the main buildings, is a more modest 1904 building housing a seven-day-a-week market with antiques and bric-a-brac on Mondays, crafts on Saturdays and Sundays, and a general market on Tuesday to Friday.

Yet another former market building, the Flower Market on the east side of the piazza, was built in 1872 and features original glass and cast-iron work. It now houses the London Transport Museum (379-6344), open daily 10 to 6; admission free up to 30 minutes—thereafter £2.40 (children £1.10). The Victoria and Albert Museum's Theater Museum (831-1227), opened next door on Shakespeare's birthday (April 23) '87 to generally favorable reviews. It's open daily, except Monday, 11 A.M. to 7 P.M.; admission £2.25, children £1.25.

Past the museum is **Joe Allen,** 13 Exeter Street (836 –0651), a bit of Manhattan in London hiding discreetly behind a brass name plate on an obscure Covent Garden back street. The vast basement room features a menu chalked on the wall offering good spare ribs, enormous salads, and well-made cocktails. Lots of showbiz and media folk who make lots of noise. Up to £25 for two.

Two blocks north is the Drury Lane Theater Royal (836-8108), which confusingly has its entrance on Catherine Street. This is an elegant Georgian building and one of London's largest theaters, used mainly for spectacular musicals. Even if you are not seeing a show there, try to get a glimpse inside the foyer of its wide staircases, high domed ceiling, and circular balcony.

Cross Russell Street onto Bow Street to see the front of the Royal Opera House (240-1066), also home of the Royal Ballet. This is a mid-19th-century building of classic design where all-night lines for tickets are not unknown.

In London the name **Bertorelli's**—44a Floral Street (836-3969)—is linked with the best in Italian restaurants. Here the family have created a chic, stylish decor and a menu that caters for those wanting a light healthy snack, a substantial lunch, or a three-course dinner. Hence simply cooked grilled Dover sole; exotic monkfish, scallops and prawns skewered and grilled with peppers; freshly made pasta and pizza; traditional dishes such as *saltimbocca alla Romagna* (escalopes of veal with Parma ham and white wine) and delicate salads. Open from noon to midnight seven days a week and can seat 170 people on three levels.

Le Cafe du Jardin 28 Wellington Street (839-8769), has created a corner of France behind its red and white gingham curtains. Watch Covent Garden's street life or escape to the sanctuary of the large basement "garden." A bistro-style menu with dishes such as *soupe à l'oignon, boeuf bourguignon* and *gigot d'agneau.* At lunch they serve a good value three-course meal at £7.95 a head, and between 5:45 and 7:15 P.M., a pre-theater menu for £6.95.

In a narrow court between Long Acre and the Opera House, another Covent Garden conversion of an old warehouse is **Le Café des Amis du Vin,** 11–14 Hanover Place (379–3444), with a downstairs wine bar, a ground floor restaurant, and a quieter upstairs "salon." Eat in the ground floor restaurant if you like a lively, noisy environment, upstairs for more sedate surroundings, and downstairs for an informal snack and a glass of wine.

This is brasserie-style dining with the day's specials chalked up on a board, and a menu offering straightforward French cooking at very reasonable prices. The fish dishes are particularly good, or try the *boudin noir*—a "black pudding" sausage from the Normandy region of France. Fine cheeses and specially imported French bread. About £18 for two.

Ajimura, 51–53 Shelton Street (240–0178), is something of a rarity in London—a Japanese restaurant that doesn't cater to big expense account customers. The restaurant contains a couple of small, plain rooms, one of them with a sushi bar ideal for lone meals and snacks.

Choose one of the set meals if you are a newcomer to Japanese food. Try a Japanese hors d'oeuvre such as marinated fish in ginger and onion, or spinach rolled in seaweed, or deep fried bean curd. Follow this with sashimi (raw fish), then grilled mackerel, and a main dish of beef Teriyaki—thin slices of beef grilled in Teriyaki sauce—all accompanied by rice, soup, and dessert. Around £20 for two. Alternatively, choose from the *à la carte* menu. Either way, wash it all down with warm sake and you'll have had a Japanese feast for a modest sum.

The streets running south from the piazza lead you to The Strand, a traffic-clogged thoroughfare parallel with the Thames and linking Trafalgar Square and Fleet Street. A fairly ordinary shopping street serving local office workers, it is notable primarily for its theaters— Adelphi, The Vaudeville, and The Savoy, and in The Aldwych crescent, The Duchess, The Strand, and The Aldwych—and The Savoy Hotel, a luxury hotel overlooking the Thames and a long-time favorite among show business people.

The area known as The Savoy, which includes the hotel, theater, and chapel, was given its name in the 13th century when there was a royal palace on the site. Since

1881 the name has been synonymous with Gilbert and Sullivan operas. These were performed at the Savoy Theatre, specially built for the purpose by Richard D'Oyly Carte, who also built the hotel. The imposing 18th-century building on the right as you come to the Aldwych is Somerset House, which now houses offices of the Inland Revenue and probate archives. The building in the middle of the Strand, created by the Aldwych semicircle, houses the BBC's World Service studios.

Simpsons-in-the-Strand, 100 The Strand (836–9112), is almost an English institution. Simpsons is the restaurant for roast beef, lamb, mutton, veal, and venison which is wheeled to your table on great silver serving trolleys and carved by waiters who are trained in the art.

Eating at Simpsons is an experience as much as a meal. Two great, high-ceilinged rooms (the ground floor for gentlemen only) are dominated by well-spaced tables with stiffly starched white tablecloths and formal English service in a style rarely found today. It's almost obligatory to try the beef, but there's also duck, or you might try tripe and onions, a favorite dish from the north of England. Finish with Stilton cheese and a glass of port. About £30 for two.

BLOOMSBURY

Bloomsbury is one of central London's quieter areas, despite the presence of some 70,000 students in the London University buildings during school sessions. There are few restaurants here, except along Charlotte Street, and no movie houses, theaters, or bright lights. Yet it contains much of interest, not least the magnificent British Museum, the small but richly-stocked Courtauld Institute Galleries, and, a little further north, the house in which Charles Dickens lived and wrote some of his best-known books.

It also has some attractive Georgian squares. Indeed, the concept of the square in town planning is said to have evolved here when, in 1661, the fourth Earl of Southampton had the idea of building houses around three sides of a square and added a mansion for himself on the fourth. That was Bloomsbury Square, followed in later years by Bedford, Russell, Tavistock, Torrington, Woburn, and Gordon Squares.

Always a fashionable area, it became identified with writers, artists, critics, philosophers, actors, and scholars at the beginning of this century, particularly the so-called Bloomsbury Group led by writer/publisher Virginia Woolf. Although for the most part it is no longer residential, the district maintains its literary links through the University and the presence of a number of publishing houses.

The British Museum, Great Russell Street (636–1555), is an awe-inspiring colonnaded building behind a giant quadrangle. Inside is an even more awe-inspiring collection that ranges from a fifth-century B.C. Caryatid (a column-like draped female figure) from the Greek Acropolis to Shakespeare's signature; from a third-century B.C. bronze head of Sophocles to the Magna Carta; from Egyptian mummies (pet animals as well as humans) to the original manuscript of *Alice In Wonderland.* You need a day or more to do it justice, or just select a few galleries and concentrate on them. Open 10 A.M. to 5 P.M. Monday to Saturday, 2:30 to 6 P.M. Sunday. Free.

The Courtauld Institute Galleries, Woburn Square (387–0370), features wonderful impressionist and post-impressionist paintings by Manet, Van Gogh, Degas, Bonnard, Gauguin, Cezanne, and Seurat from the private collection of Samuel Courtauld. There are also some primitive and Renaissance works, the Roger Fry bequest (Bloomsbury Group), sculptures, and portraits. Open 10 A.M. to 5 P.M. Monday to Saturday, 2 to 5 P.M. Sunday. Admission: £1.50, children 50p.

Dickens House, 48 Doughty Street (405–2127). Arguably London's most famous writer, Charles Dickens lived in this 18th-century terraced house for three years between 1837 and 1839. He completed *Pickwick Papers* and wrote *Nicholas Nickleby* and *Oliver Twist* here. You can see many of his original manuscripts, letters, mementos, and family portraits. Open 10 A.M. to 4:30 P.M. Monday to Saturday. Admission: £1.50, children 50p.

Pizza Express, 30 Coptic Street (636-3232), is handy for the British Museum. Housed in a converted dairy, the restaurant retains much of the original tile-work. Delicious, generously topped Italian pizzas are cooked before your eyes and served with flourish. Branches dotted around London are of a consistent standard. A drink and a pizza averages £4.

West End

The West End is what Londoners call their downtown area, but it has no set boundaries in a geographical sense. It is generally accepted as the main shopping/dining/ entertainment district of central London. To any British person the "West End" conjures to mind bright lights, smart shops, and glamour.

For present purposes the West End roughly encompasses Oxford Street, Regent Street, Trafalgar Square, and Charing Cross Road, taking in Soho, Leicester Square, and Piccadilly Circus.

The heart of the West End, indeed the pulse of London, is Piccadilly Circus. Although allowed to become somewhat sleazy in the last decade, redevelopment is helping to clean up the area. The view at night with the glass and neon advertising signs remains exciting, nonetheless.

At center is the statue of Eros—god of love. The monument is a memorial to Lord Shaftesbury, a Victorian philanthropist who campaigned for legislation to improve the lot of the poor during the industrial revolution. Eros is set on a paved traffic island from which six of the city's best known streets radiate—Piccadilly, leading west to Hyde Park; the sweeping crescent of Regent Street and its fine shops; Shaftesbury Avenue and its theaters; Coventry Street, leading to Leicester Square; Haymarket; and Lower Regent Street, with its distant views to Westminster.

The days when traffic completely encircled Eros are long over thanks to a combination of traffic congestion and the need to protect tourists risking life and limb to reach his island. After 40 years of debate, 1986 saw Eros moved south to link with the Criterion block, thus allowing pedestrians unhindered access to the cleaned and repaired statue.

To tour the West End, walk up Regent Street, a wide, curving thoroughfare designed in the early 1800s by architect John Nash who, with builder and developer Thomas Cubitt, was responsible for many of London's elegant Regency terraces.

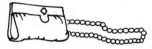

One of London's prime shopping streets, Regent Street's broad expanse, wide sidewalks, and fashionable shops make it a pleasant stroll. The main shops are:

The Scotch House (84–86)—woolens, tartans, etc.; **Aquascutum** (100)—classy clothes store, reverential atmosphere, steep prices; **Austin Reed** (103)—traditional men's clothes, now for women, too; **Garrard** (112)—highly respected for gold and silver, rings, etc.; **Wilson & Gill** (137)—Rosenthal china; **Lawleys** (154)—china; **Gered Wedgwood** (158)—china by Wedgwood, Spode, Coalport; **Mappin & Webb** (170)—high-class china and glassware; **Regent Textiles** (179–181)—one of several Regent Street shops selling lengths of cloth and offering tax-free arrangements for overseas customers; **Hamleys** (188)—said to be the biggest toy shop in the world; **Jaeger** (200–206)—distinctive designs in clothes for men and women; **Laura Ashley** (208)—extensive range of original print dresses, fabric, etc., reasonably priced; **Liberty** (214–222)—world-renowned department store with eye-catching, mock-Tudor front and pleasantly old-fashioned in its merchandise and demeanor. Good for its own prints in materials and dresses, also men's clothes, jewelry, art, books, and gifts; **Dickins & Jones** (224)—solid, middle-class department store.

The Criterion Brasserie, 222 Piccadilly (839–7133), is without a doubt the most beautiful place to eat out in Leicester Square. Do look up at the ceiling when you visit: it's gold mosaic inlaid with semi-precious stones and is the crowning glory of a neo-Byzantine marble hall. The front of the vast restaurant is run as a brasserie with its own inexpensive menu which ranges from croissant to smoked salmon. Drinks can be taken at the long bar while the main restaurant offers a short menu of modern dishes and popular classical French food. Best, though, are the char-grilled fish and meat for lunch or dinner; otherwise take advantage of the no-minimum-charge policy at the front. A proper meal will cost £30 for two.

Restorative oysters can be enjoyed at the bar in the very atmospheric **Bentley's,** 11–15 Swallow Street (734–4756), somewhat hidden away in a street that curves down from Regent Street into Piccadilly. The bar is marble topped and Bentley's oyster men are adept at their job; follow up with another British fish classic such as smoked haddock topped with poached egg, or grilled Dover sole. From £15 a head. More informal, and cheaper, too, is a wine bar in the basement.

It is quite likely that there will be an opportunity to spot some stars at **Le Tire Bouchon,** 6 Upper James Street (437–5348), located as it is very close to Granada TV's offices. It's a cosy little place with a simple menu that relies on good produce and is essentially a snack menu with dishes such as smoked country ham, crisp interesting salads, superb French cheeses, mussels and garlicky prawns. It is very, very busy at lunchtime but is also open for breakfast, tea, and early suppers. Closed Sat. and Sun.

* * *

Just before Oxford Circus, where Regent Street bi-sects Oxford Street, turn right at Great Marlborough Street, then left onto Argyll Street for the London Pal-ladium. This is probably London's best-known theater due to its televised variety shows and to solo perform-ances by top American stars. It is now the home of long-running musicals.

North of Oxford Circus, the white '30s-style build-ing is Broadcasting House, home of the British Broad-casting Corporation (BBC). To its right is John Nash's Church of All Souls, constructed in 1822.

Stretching left and right is Oxford Street, probably second only to Tokyo's Ginza as the world's busiest shopping street. Most of the big chain stores have a flag-ship outlet on Oxford Street, but there are also many rubbishy shops to be avoided at all costs. In recent years Oxford Street has been banned to private motor traffic and the sidewalks have been widened, but there are still enough buses, taxis, and vans to clog it and make cross-ing the street dangerous.

Earmark another time to return to "do" Oxford Street, rather than on this tour; when you do, you'll find the best shops in the section from Oxford Circus west to Marble Arch.

The best of the stores:
Marks & Spencer (173 and 458 Oxford Street), re-nowned for the quality of men's, women's, and children's clothing, and for its imaginative food, and for refunding money without question as long as you return the goods purchased in their bag with a receipt.

Selfridges takes up a whole block between Orchard and Duke Streets. One of the great stores of the world, founded by Gordon Selfridge in 1908, it's architecturally interesting with its Ionic columns, and it stocks a wide range of items, particularly food, teenage fashions, gifts, and perfumes.

John Lewis, occupying the block between Old Cavendish Street and Holles Street, insists it will be "never knowingly undersold." If you find an item selling for less elsewhere, the store will match the price. Good for clothes and household items.

The HMV Shop (150 and 363 Oxford Street) and **Tower Records** (1 Piccadilly) feature an enormous range of records, tapes, and video cassettes, equalled only by **The Virgin Megastore,** 14–16 Oxford Street, which has a wider selection of rock music. Upstairs with a balcony overlooking the Megastore is a fast order **Cafe.** The menu is international with dishes as diverse as fresh pasta (around £2), various American sandwiches (from £2.50 to £2.75), salads and simple substantial dishes such as char-grilled steak and veal sausage. Liquor license but only for those eating. Open 9 A.M. until 11.30 P.M. Mon. to Sat.

Continuing the tour, turn right along Oxford Street at Oxford Circus and hurry along this fairly boring stretch to the junction with Tottenham Court Road (mainly hi-fi and video shops, but take a detour to Heals/ Habitat at No. 196 if you are interested in the latest in home-furnishing ideas) and turn right down Charing Cross Road. Note one of London's few skyscrapers, Centre Point, on the left.

Charing Cross Road is synonymous with bookshops, the best-known of which is Foyles (No. 119), well stocked on even the most obscure subject, but not a place to browse or in which to shop comfortably. Waterstones (No. 121) is one of a new breed of bookshops with pleasant, helpful assistants, carpeted floors, classical music, and wide gangways. They stay open late while most bookstores close at 6 P.M.

Further along Charing Cross Road—past Cambridge Circus, dominated by the Palace Theatre—there is Zwemmer (No. 76–80) for art and architecture books. There are also several second-hand bookshops.

Just off to the left on West Street is the St. Martin's Theatre where Agatha Christie's *The Mousetrap* is now in its 35th year—the world's longest theater run. It is inevitable, now, that the performance is run-of-the-mill, but still worth seeing as a kind of living museum piece.

The block from Charing Cross Road down to Cranbourn Street has bookshops, but save some time for the specialty book stores on St. Martin's and Cecil Courts, to the left past Wyndham's Theatre.

Cafe Pelican, 45 St. Martin's Lane (379-0309), is very close to a French brasserie. Take tea at one of the pavement tables, snack at the long bar, lunch at one of the many front tables, or enjoy a three-course meal in the restaurant at the rear. Open 11–2 A.M. and is the perfect place to imagine for a moment that you are on the other side of the channel. *Saucisson, pâté* and bread; *croque monsieur* and other snacks average £3 while a set luncheon of steak and *frites* costs under £10 a head. Ambitious modern French cooking—which can vary wildly in quality—served in the restaurant averages £15 a head.

Sheekey's, 28 St. Martin's Court (240–2565) is a long-established, solid, and comfortable fish restaurant, a favorite among theatergoers for a hundred years or more. Three dining rooms are wood paneled, walls are lined with signed photos of thespians, and there is a relaxed atmosphere.

If you are feeling adventurous, experiment with a typical Cockney London dish—stewed eels with mashed potatoes or Sheekey's specialties: shrimp scampi cooked in tarragon and white wine, then glazed and served with noodles; or sole poached in white wine with noodles. The menu has many other varieties of fish including lobster and turbot, and, of course, the oysters, in season, are impeccable. There are also some meat dishes. About £40 for two.

Your walk through Cecil Court will bring you out in St. Martin's Lane, which has the Albery and Duke of York Theatres and the London Coliseum, home of the English National Opera Company.

Beotys, 79 St. Martin's Lane (836–8768), is a useful theater-district Greek restaurant, nicely old-fashioned with plush red banquettes and charming service. Reliable Greek Cypriot cooking includes moussaka, souvlaki, and squid in red wine. Sweet and sticky Greek desserts, good coffee, and a complimentary box of Turkish delight finish off every meal! About £25 for two.

Turn right down St. Martin's Lane and you will join Charing Cross Road again at the main Post Office (open 8 to 8 Monday to Saturday, 10 to 5 Sunday). Before you will be the National Gallery, with the magnificent vista of Trafalgar Square opening up ahead. Atop the 185-foot column at the center of the square stands Lord Nelson, England's most heroic admiral in the French revolutionary wars. He died in the Battle of Trafalgar as his men destroyed the French fleet.

The 20-foot-long, 11-foot-high lions at the foot of the column are by Sir Edwin Landseer; the fountains behind the monument are floodlit at night and a focal point for traditional New Year's revelry. At Christmas a tree—a gift from Norway—is erected in the square and there are nightly carol services; on weekends the square is often used for political rallies.

Standing on the splendid terrace of the National Gallery, you will view Whitehall, with its government offices leading down to Westminster, and Admiralty Arch, the beginning of The Mall; on the other end of The Mall is Buckingham Palace. On the right is Canada House; to the left, a statue of George Washington. Farther left is the church of St. Martin-in-the-Fields, and Charing Cross Station.

The National Gallery (839–3321) was built in 1838 to complement Nash's square and to house an art collection founded in 1824 by Parliamentary purchase of 38 pictures brought together by a City merchant banker. Today the 40-odd rooms contain over 2,000 paintings, from 13th-century Italian to 19th-century French works. The collection includes Dutch, Flemish, German, and Spanish paintings, and, of course, masterpieces of the 17th- and 18th-century British painters such as Constable and Turner. Open 10 A.M. to 6 P.M. Monday to Saturday, 2 to 6 P.M. Sunday. Free.

At the rear of the building, with a separate entrance in St. Martin's Place, is the National Portrait Gallery (930 –1552), open 10 A.M. to 5 P.M. Monday to Friday, 10 A.M. to 6 P.M. Saturday, 2 to 6 P.M. Sunday. A fascinating history of the British is told here in portraits of the famous—from Royalty to theater personalities—chosen as revelations of character, not necessarily because of their merit as works of art. Four floors are packed with faces including those of Henry VII, George Bernard Shaw, Shakespeare, W.H. Auden, Princess Diana.

Upon leaving the National Portrait Gallery, walk left along Irving Street into green and leafy Leicester Square. On the fringes of the square are London's major cinemas. It's also an area of fast-food restaurants and a slightly sleazy atmosphere, though refurbishment of some buildings on the north side is improving its appearance.

This is the beginning of Soho, once the site of appalling slums. It is an area that has attracted a cosmopolitan population of refugees over the years who brought with them their native cuisine and traditions of service. The result was that Soho became London's main restaurant district, and still is, to a large extent. Unfortunately, prostitution, porno shops, and sleazy sex clubs also moved in, and campaigns to clean up the area never seem to succeed completely.

There's a Chinatown section around Gerrard Street with several excellent restaurants, notably **Dragon Gate** at No. 7 (734–5154), **The Dumpling Inn** at No. 15a (437–2567), and **Lido** at No. 41 (437–4431). Look in on the vast **New World** around the corner at 1 Gerrard Place (734-0677); like its parent **Chuen Cheng Ku** at 17 Wardour Street (437-1398) it is excellent for the Chinese snack meal of *dim sum* served until about 6 P.M. at many restaurants in Soho's Chinatown. All can be relied upon for good-quality Chinese food in authentic surroundings. Unlike some other Chinatown districts, this one is perfectly safe to walk in at night.

Soho spreads north from Shaftesbury Avenue to Oxford Street and includes the film industry offices on Wardour Street, colorful street markets on Rupert and Berwick, and Ronnie Scott's jazz club on Frith. It may surprise many Americans to learn that television was invented here on Frith Street, at No. 23a, by a Scotsman called John Logie Baird.

The Chicago Meatpackers, 96 Charing Cross Road (379-3277), can seat 300 in its basement dining room. Decorated with railway signs and a miniature railway running above diners' heads, it's the ideal place to take young children. The food is American: burgers, Butch McGuir's roast pork and other sandwiches, and excellent barbecued ribs. Don't miss Hilary's onion loaf, like an onion bhaji and a meal in itself. Three courses average £12 a head.

Compton Green, 14 Old Compton Street (434-3544), is quite unlike any of London's other vegetarian restaurants. It looks more like a fashionable brasserie (of which there are several in Soho) and successfully proves that vegetarian restaurants don't have to sport rattan lampshades and serve nut cutlets. Here you hardly notice that there's no meat in the food: avocado with tofu and lemon mayonnaise; marinated vegetables and tofu kebab with noodles, peanut sauce and broccoli, to give you an idea. Bread is homemade, puddings and cakes sugar free, and the wine list is long and varied. Bright and breezy, with young and trendy staff and food that's unusual yet delicious. Inexpensive too, at around £5 per person.

The Gay Hussar, 2 Greek Street (437–0973), is a Soho survivor and favorite among politicians and the media people. Rich Hungarian cooking at its best is served in a cramped but cozy old-fashioned room that is slightly formal but enlivened by friendly waiters. Good soups, including chilled sour cherry, and hefty portions of goulash, chicken with peppers, jugged hare (a kind of stewed rabbit), or brill with onions. There's a set three-course lunch at £8, but for a la carte expect to pay around £30 for two.

Kettners, 29 Romilly Street (437–6437), is perhaps the smartest pizza joint in the world. Once one of London's classiest restaurants, Kettners is now owned by the Pizza Express chain, which has retained the chintzy atmosphere complete with champagne bar and separate cocktail bar with pianist. The restaurant is elegant but the food is inexpensive and the usual range of pizzas live up to the quality of the surroundings. You could eat a pizza for less than £3, but a full meal for two would come to about £19.

Soho Brasserie, 23–25 Old Compton Street (439–9301), is one of the most fashionable places in Soho; it is a multipurpose converted pub, and offers a breakfast menu and a bar menu, with a comprehensive range of alcoholic and non-alcoholic drinks. At its rear there is a small restaurant that serves good modern French food. During the summer the open windows make it feel like a Parisian cafe, even if it is in the heart of Soho. Snack for under £5 a head or enjoy a three-course meal for around £15 a head.

Mayfair

Mayfair is what the English call "posh." It's filled with the best and most expensive hotels, restaurants, shops, and galleries; large squares with immaculate gardens; elegant, well-maintained town houses and apartment buildings; and still a few residents able to afford the high rates and rents, though probably there are as many business sheikhs from the petrodollar-rich Middle East countries as there were English nobility and merchants who made their homes here a century ago.

Mayfair is neatly contained by Oxford Street, Park Lane, Piccadilly, and Regent Street. To the south of Piccadilly, in an L-shaped corner between Green and St. James's parks, is the St. James's district, possibly even more exclusive than Mayfair with St. James's Palace and Clarence House (home of Queen Elizabeth, the Queen Mother), the Ritz Hotel, Jermyn Street's top drawer men's shops, and the gentlemen's clubs of Pall Mall and St. James's Street.

At the extreme northwest corner of Mayfair is Marble Arch, originally designed by John Nash as an entrance to Buckingham Palace, but transposed to this site in 1851. It is one of central London's busiest junctions,

where Oxford Street meets the Edgware Road heading
north, Bayswater Road heading west, and Park Lane
going south. The triumphal arch, which is indeed made
of marble, sits grandly in the middle of this great traffic
circle decorated by lawns and fountains.

Park Lane has some of London's most desirable
property, with uninterrupted views of the lush green expanse of Hyde Park. But the five-star hotels along here
are relatively modern—Grosvenor House, which fills an
entire block, and the Dorchester, with its fairy-light trees
and fountain, were built in 1930; the London Hilton, Inn
On The Park, Londonderry, and Intercontinental were
all built within the last 20 years.

Walking along Park Lane from Marble Arch, turn
left after two blocks onto Upper Brook Street.

Le Gavroche, 43 Upper Brook Street (730–2820), is
one of London's acknowledged top restaurants, with
prices to match. Expect to pay up to £90 for two at dinner
(or £20 each for the set luncheon menu). You can be
assured of the food which has all the restaurant guides
and food writers reaching for their superlatives. There is
a bar on the ground floor; the restaurant is downstairs in
a formal room with Chagalls adorning the walls. Jackets
and ties—if not formal dress—are definitely encouraged.

One of London's master chefs, Albert Roux, runs Le
Gavroche, and the cuisine is just about as haute as you
can go. Among the dishes that you may be offered are
Dublin Bay prawns in a tomato, herb, white wine, and
brandy sauce, a house specialty souffle, truffle mousse,
beef filet in grapes, or a mixed seafood stew in vermouth
sauce. If you can manage it, finish with the *assiette du chef*
—a sliver of each dessert from the trolley.

You will be eating in good company at the Gavroche
—it's beloved by government officials and diplomats
from the nearby American Embassy. (The Embassy itself,
incidentally, is an impressive modern building, crowned
by a gold eagle, occupying the entire west side of Gros-

venor Square. It has a pleasant green garden where you will find a memorial to Franklin D. Roosevelt. Most of the buildings round about are U.S. State Department offices.)

The lower ranking officials from the U.S. Embassy and offices eat at **Justin de Blank's** self-service restaurant at 54 Duke Street (629–3174), which might be described as a fast-food cafe, inasmuch as it's not a place to linger. Lines hover waiting for your table, but there the similarity with a hamburger joint ends. Everything is fresh and freshly cooked—soups, pates, casseroles, vegetarian dishes, and a good range of desserts. Just the place for a quick but satisfying lunch after shopping in nearby Oxford Street or during your tour of Mayfair. It shouldn't cost you more than £12 for two. (No credit cards.)

Continuing down Duke Street, past Grosvenor Square and into Carlos Place, you'll find the **Connaught Hotel** (corner of Mount Street). Favored by Hollywood stars, the Connaught is one of London's stateliest hotels —a late 19th-century grey stone building with a pillared entrance and magnificent carved wood staircase. Along Brook Street, leading east from Grosvenor Square, is one of London's other grand hotels, **Claridges,** which is frequented by visiting heads of state.

If you continue along Brook Street, on the left you will come to South Molton Street, a short, paved, pedestrian block that has become fashionable in recent years as a sort of younger people's version of nearby Bond Street—and definitely up-market from Oxford Street, which joins it. Chic clothes shops for men and women.

Widow Applebaum's, 46 South Molton Street (629–4649). In summer you can sit outside at this (almost) authentic American deli and watch the boutique shoppers. Pastrami on rye, bacon, lettuce, and tomato sandwiches, etc. About £15 for two (no credit cards).

Brook Street brings you out in the middle of New Bond/Old Bond streets, the smart shopping street with everything from Gucci shoes to handmade chocolates, from Sotheby's world-famous auction rooms to the shop that supplies the Queen's notepaper. Among the highlights, beginning on New Bond Street:

Russell & Bromley (24 and 109)—quality shoes; **Tessiers** (25–26)—gold and silver; **Sotheby's** (34)—world-renowned auction house; **Fogal** (36)—men's and women's hose; **F. Pinet** (47) and **Kurt Geiger** (95 and 114)—classy shoes; **Smythsons** (54)—stationery and notepaper, as supplied to Her Majesty The Queen; **Fenwick** (63)—reasonably priced fashion department store, primarily for women; **Bond Street Antique Centre** (124) —supermarket-like atmosphere with 44 antique shops, high prices; **Herbie Frogg** (125)—exclusive men's clothes; **S. J. Phillips** (139)—antique silver; **Polo Ralph Lauren** (143)—you know . . . him; **Partridge** (144–146) —fine arts; **Wildenstein** (147)—historic building (once the house of Lord Nelson), selling paintings and drawings; **Louis Vuitton** (149)—leathergoods and baggage; **Ireland House Shops** (150)—Irish linen, crystal, knitwear; **Van Cleef & Arpels** (153)—the jewelers; **Asprey** (165–169)—London's Tiffany's, with jewels, antiques, porcelain, silver, gifts; **Cartier** (175)—the jewelers.

On Old Bond Street:

Arthur Ackerman (3)—established 1783, sells fine

sporting prints and paintings; **Booty Jewelry** (9)—interesting items by new designers; **Pierre Cardin** (20)—the French designer of men's and women' wear; **Chanel** (26)—ladies designer clothes from France; **Gucci** (27)—leather goods, gifts, etc.; **Charbonnel & Walker** (28)—handmade chocolates; **Thomas Agnew & Sons** (43)—fine art dealers; **Ciro** (48)—jewelry.

On Cork Street you'll find a wealth of galleries for the wealthy, including **Bernard Jacobson** (2a), **Waddington** (2), **Nicola Jacobs** (9), **Browse & Darby,** (19) and **Redfern** (20). Upper Brook Street is home to a variety of designer shops for women, among which are **Guy Laroche** (33); **Roland Klein** (26); **Emanuel** (26), where Princess Diana had her wedding dress fashioned and where advance appointments are necessary (call 629–5569); and **Courtenay** (22–24)—for distinctive ladies' separates and lingerie.

Browse, also, along the surrounding streets—Mount, Albemarle, and Conduit streets, Burlington Gardens, and Sackville Street for antique shops, more fashion stores, and commercial art galleries. Savile Row is known worldwide for its men's tailors (made-to-measure suits start at around £500); 3 Savile Row is also to be noted as the house where, at the height of their fame, the Beatles had their headquarters.

Parallel with Old Bond Street, leading to Piccadilly, is the Burlington Arcade, a not-to-be-missed early 19th-century arcade of fascinating shops selling jewelry, tobacco, pipes, cashmere sweaters, and gifts in a unique setting. There's even a beadle in uniform to shut the gates and keep order.

Adjacent, in Piccadilly, is Burlington House (734–9052). Set back from the road in its own courtyard, it dates from the 17th century and now houses the Royal Academy of Arts and its galleries. The RA summer exhibition (May to August) is a leading event in the London social calendar, when hundreds of paintings and sculptures are exhibited and sold. There's also a major exhibition of some kind during the winter, and other events throughout the year. Open daily from 10 A.M. to 6 P.M. Admission varies, depending on the exhibition.

Piccadilly runs from Piccadilly Circus west to Hyde Park Corner and borders Green Park for half its length. The street name derives from a tailor who specialized in making pickadills—frilly lace things worn by the Elizabethans—and who amassed enough money to build a mansion, Pickadill Hall, near where the Circus now stands.

Much of Piccadilly is today taken up with airline offices, car showrooms, hotels, and some imposing Georgian buildings that house offices and men's clubs. Piccadilly's best-known shop is **Fortnum and Mason** (181 Piccadilly, 734–8040), a top-class shop noted primarily for its foods but also handling clothing and gifts. Here tailcoated salesmen will take your order for a packet of tea or a brace of pheasant. The store also has a delightful restaurant, The Fountain, a very English sort of place, great for afternoon tea or a light pre-theater meal. It stays open until 11:30 P.M., long after the store has closed. **Hatchards** (187) is London's premier bookshop with an efficient staff who know their stock.

Some fine restaurants are to be found off on the side streets emanating from Piccadilly:

Pappagalli's Pizzas, 7–9 Swallow Street, just off Piccadilly at the Circus end (734–5182), serves Sicilian deep dish pizzas in an unusual Gothic churchy setting. They also offer pasta and salads, plus a variety of cocktails and American beer. Recommended as a good, cheap meal in the heart of the West End, especially handy before or after the theater. Around £15 for two.

Langan's Brasserie, Stratton Street, just off Piccadilly (493–6437), is a decidedly upscale place, needing reservations days ahead, especially for lunch. Despite the vast size of its main ground floor room where the glitterati of society, show business, and the media come to dine, see, and be seen, the food's actually pretty good. The restaurant's namesake is Peter Langan, a gossip column character himself with a reputation for downing a bottle of champagne a day. If he's in London, you'll find him eating here, too, as well as part owner Michael Caine.

It is almost obligatory, on your first visit, to have the spinach souffle with anchovy sauce starter, but the closely hand-written menu lists no less than 29 offerings and as many *plats du jour*, so you won't be stuck for choice. Quails eggs in pastry, seafood salad, and assorted smoked fish in horseradish sauce are other recommended starters. Follow with veal in herb butter, trout braised with cucumbers or pan-fried herring in mustard sauce. Good plain roasts and grills are also available. About £50 for two but worth it. Less frenetic in the evening and in the smaller upstairs dining rooms.

The Hard Rock Cafe, 150 Old Park Lane, with its entrance on Piccadilly at the Hyde Park end (629–0382), is incongruously set at the more dignified end of Piccadilly. This spot gave London its first taste of proper American hamburgers back in the late '60s, and it still has the best reputation around for that. Indeed, customers wait in line on the street for a table. Loud music, cocktails, and all the usual variations of burgers and similar American bar food. Around £15 for two (no credit cards).

Just to the north of Piccadilly behind the Hard Rock Cafe is an area of small criss-crossed streets with antique shops, pubs, and restaurants. Known as Shepherd's Market, it is worth a detour to browse through the shops. Have a drink at the **Shepherd's Tavern,** 50 Hertford Street (499–3017), a bow-windowed pub with a telephone in a sedan chair reputedly used by the Duke of Cumberland (the chair, that is).

L'Artiste Musclé, 1 Shepherd Market (493–6150), is a tiny corner bistro with bare wood tables that is justifiably popular with local office workers for lunch, and with moviegoers (the luxurious Curzon Cinema is nearby) at night. They all come for juicy steak reeking of herbs and garlic, crisp salad with French dressing, crusty French bread, soft brie, and a bottle of Rhone wine. Around £15 for two.

The Mayfair district actually began here in Shepherd's Market, thanks to architect Edward Shepherd who took over the site of an annual May market and fair in

1735, opened a food market, and built a housing development. Today the Shepherd's Market area has a reputation as a red-light district, but don't let that stop your visiting this picturesque corner of London.

South of Piccadilly is Green Park, a peaceful oasis away from the traffic and bustle, which runs down to Buckingham Palace. It is a favorite lunchtime picnic spot for office workers in the summer. Its proper name is The Green Park, and it's just that—a natural park of grass with a wide variety of trees. On the corner of the park by Piccadilly is yet another of London's grand hotels, The Ritz, a solid Edwardian building with lavish decorations and the best cucumber sandwiches and afternoon tea in London.

Running down the side of The Ritz is St. James's Street, the main thoroughfare of the St. James's district, which is encompassed by Haymarket, Piccadilly, The Mall, and Green Park. At the time of Charles II, this was an exclusive residential area for courtiers. Later many of the houses became men's clubs, some of which remain today. Note White's (37) dating from 1693, Boodle's (28), and Brooks (61). Locks (6) is a shop specializing in top hats and bowlers. Berry Bros. & Rudd (3), with its shuttered windows, is a fine old wine merchant.

Le Caprice, Arlington House (629–2239). At the foot of a cul-de-sac street parallel with St. James, on the ground floor of an office and apartment building, this smallish art deco restaurant attracts a fashionable clientele (even the younger members of the Royal Family, as well as the latest rock stars). But the prices are not excessive and the food is good international fare. Particularly fine *crudités* or leek tart make the best starters. Three meats (beef, lamb, and veal) are served with a Dijon sauce. There is also a steak tartare, spiced to taste, and a choice of fish dishes. Interesting desserts can be accompanied by a glass of sweet dessert wine. About £35 for two.

Jermyn Street, running from St. James's Street, parallel with Piccadilly, has exclusive men's shoe shops such as **Trickers** (67) and shirt shops including **Turnbull & Asser** (71) and **Harvie & Hudson** (77, 96 and 97). You may also want to have a sniff around **Paxton & Whitfield's** famous cheese shop at 93. If you *are* a cheese person, drool over their incredible range of English cheeses, even though it's not practical to buy any to take home!

North of the Oxford Street edge of Mayfair is the Marylebone district, developed from the St. Marylebone village in the early 18th century and containing Georgian houses in its three principal squares—Cavendish, Portman, and Manchester. Here, also, is Baker Street, where Arthur Conan Doyle's famous fictitious detective, Sherlock Holmes, had his chambers at 221B. Don't bother to make the trip—it's a very plain office building.

But Marylebone has one of London's most-visited tourist attractions—Madame Tussaud's Waxworks, and the lesser-visited, but arguably more worthwhile, Wallace Collection.

Madame Tussaud's, Marylebone Road (486–1121). Whether you spend time standing in line, then shuffling round the invariably overcrowded Madame Tussaud's, depends on how fascinating you find the idea of famous and infamous characters from history and the present day modeled with mostly uncanny lifelike precision in wax. They change the inmates to keep up with who's still topical (imagine the ignominy of being a melted-down ex-waxwork).

There really was a Madame Tussaud, a French lady born in 1761 who moved from Paris to England in 1802, traveling the country with her own hand-made waxwork models before setting up in Marylebone in 1835. Open 10 A.M. (9:30 at weekends) to 5:30 P.M. daily. Admission: £3.95; £2.50 for children. Next door is the London

Planetarium with its visual display of the night sky. There are regular star show presentations between 11 A.M. and 5 P.M. every day. Open 11 A.M. (10:20 at weekends) to 5:40 P.M. Admission £2.20 (£1.40 for children). Tickets for both the waxworks and the Planetarium at £5.50; £3.10 for children.

The Wallace Collection, Hertford House, Manchester Square (935–0687), features a superb collection of paintings and antiques put together by the 19th-century Marquess of Hertford, Richard Wallace. The museum's holdings include works by 18th-century French painters Fragonard and Boucher, plus paintings by Turner, Canaletto, Van Dyck, and Rubens, along with 17th- and 18th-century French furniture, bronzes, miniatures, armor, and clocks. The Wallace Collection is open 10 A.M. to 5 P.M. Monday to Saturday; 2 P.M. to 5 P.M. Sunday. Admission is free.

Buckingham Palace Area

There is only one way to approach Buckingham Palace in order to enjoy the full majesty of its position and the grandeur of its architecture: walking from Trafalgar Square, passing through Admiralty Arch, then along The Mall—the traditional processional route from the Palace to St. Paul's Cathedral or Whitehall and Westminster.

On the left of the Mall is St. James's Park, which takes its name from a hospice founded in the 13th century for 14 poor leprous maidens. The grounds were later acquired by Henry VIII as a deerpark and garden for his new palace of St. James. It is, today, a very pleasant park for a gentle stroll and perhaps a picnic by the lake with its ducks, gulls, swans, and geese.

On the right is the rear of Carlton House Terrace, designed by John Nash in the early 19th century. Part of Carlton House is home to the Institute of Contemporary Arts (ICA, Nash House No. 12; 930-0493). Check for exhibitions in its gallery and art movies in its theater.

Further along on the right, behind the trees, is St. James's Palace, which is still the statutory seat of the sovereign, and where foreign ambassadors to London are accredited "to the court of St. James." The white buildings next door are Clarence House, also designed by Nash and home of the Queen Mother, and Lancaster House, built for the Duke of York in 1825 and now used for government conferences.

As you draw near to the Palace itself see if the Royal Standard is flying from the topmost flagpole. If so, it means that the Queen is in residence. This is the London home for her and for her immediate family; all the royal children have been raised here, and Prince Charles lived here right up until his wedding to Lady Diana.

Immediately in front of the Palace, on the central traffic island, is the Queen Victoria Memorial, 82-feet high and an excellent spot from which to photograph the Palace and The Mall. On royal occasions, when the Queen and her family appear on the balcony of the Palace, the memorial is engulfed in a sea of people stretching back from the railings several hundred yards along The Mall.

Buckingham Palace is one of London's great free attractions; there's a feel of pageantry and royal history in the air, although some find the building itself, set back from the road behind a vast forecourt, a little disappointing.

Its history takes you back to 1703 when the land here was a mulberry garden granted to the Duke of Buckingham by Queen Anne. He built a town residence and called it Buckingham House. Sixty years later, George III bought it for his Queen, Charlotte, and renamed it Queen's house. The next king, George IV, asked Nash to enlarge it, but the architect retired before it was completed. The additional construction was eventually finished by Edward Blore in 1837.

The first monarch to live in the redesigned and renamed Buckingham Palace was Queen Victoria. Work nonetheless continued on enlarging it, creating the quadrangle that the four wings now enclose. The palace as it stands today was "completed" in 1912, when the front was heightened and refaced in Portland stone.

The palace is guarded by sentries of one of five regiments of Foot Guards. The changing of the guard ceremony (daily at 11:30 A.M. in the summer, alternate days in winter), complete with marching band (except when it's raining), is one of London's most popular sights. It's your chance to see something of the pomp and circumstance of an English royal occasion. But be warned: you'll be sharing that experience with hundreds of fellow tourists. Arrive early for a good view along the railings, or from the steps on the Victoria Memorial.

None of the royal apartments are open to the public, but you can visit the Queen's Gallery (930–4832) in Buckingham Palace Road, which has a changing exhibition of works from the Royal Collection. It is closed between exhibitions, so check first. Open Tuesday to Saturday 10:30 A.M. to 5 P.M.; Sunday and public holidays. 2 to 5 P.M. Admission is £1.10. You can also visit The Royal Mews (Buckingham Palace Road), the stables and coach houses of the palace. Featured is an exhibition of state carriages, including the glass coach used for royal weddings, and reputed to be desperately uncomfortable. Open Wednesday and Thursday 2 P.M. to 4 P.M. Admission: 40p.

From Buckingham Palace walk back through St. James's Park, or along Birdcage Walk (so named because of aviaries that Charles II had ranged along this side of the Park) to Westminster.

Just before reaching Parliament Square, visit the Cabinet War Rooms (930–6961) at the corner of Horse Guards Road and Great George Street, opened on a regular basis for the first time in 1984. A maze of 150 underground rooms, 16 of them open to the public, this is where government ministers and Chiefs of Staff masterminded British war tactics from 1938 to 1945. The most famous room is the office-cum-bedroom used by Winston Churchill. In the Transatlantic Telephone Room, Churchill made many calls to President Roosevelt. Open daily from 10 A.M. to 5:15 P.M. Admission £2.50 (£1.25 for under 16s).

A statue of Sir Winston Churchill stands in the middle of Parliament Square. From it you can view the Houses of Parliament (or Palace of Westminster, as the buildings housing the House of Commons and House of Lords are officially known), the Big Ben clock tower (to be absolutely factual, only the chiming bell is called Big

Ben, not the tower itself), and Westminster Abbey. The best view of the Houses of Parliament—particularly for photographers—is from Westminster Bridge, or the Albert Embankment on the opposite side of the river.

The largely "Gothic" parliament buildings date from the middle of the last century when almost total rebuilding was carried out after a disastrous fire in 1834. (The Commons building was partly rebuilt again after World War II bombing.) In the 11th century, the site was originally a royal residence for Edward the Confessor. His palace was embellished over the years and rebuilt after numerous fires. Westminster Hall, St. Stephen's Crypt, and St. Stephen's Cloister are all that remain from those early days.

Various monarchs lived in the palace until the fire of 1512, but it was as early as 1332 that representatives of local communities, or commons, began to meet there as a "house of commons." Thus was "the Mother of Parliaments" born.

To witness the process of government today in the Strangers' Gallery of the House of Commons or House of Lords, join the line at the St. Stephens Porch when Parliament is in session (usually Monday through Thursday, 4:30 to 10 P.M. and Friday 9:30 A.M. to 3 P.M., but call 219-4272 to check). Because of limited seating, many more are turned away than get admitted. Still, it's worth trying for a chance to view the historic debating chamber, although the debates themselves may be less than exciting.

The afternoons tend to be most crowded. However, from 6 P.M. on there are usually no lines, and there are fewer people with prearranged passes from their district MPs, embassies, or consulates, which allow admission to Prime Minister's Question Time at 2:30 P.M. Friday mornings are also generally less crowded. When Parliament is not in session, visits are limited to Saturdays (10 A.M. to 5 P.M.), bank holidays, and some other days in August and September (call the number above to check).

Inside, you'll find Westminster Hall, with its original 14th-century hammerbeam roof. Here, Richard II, Sir Thomas More, Charles I, and Guy Fawkes (whose "gunpowder plot" was nearly successful in blowing up the House of Lords) stood trial.

Westminster Abbey, Broad Sanctuary (call 222–5152), is another among London's world-famous sights. The name Westminster derives from "minster in the west," as opposed to St. Paul's Cathedral, which was the minster in the east at the time when Edward the Confessor built a church to house his tomb on the site of the present Abbey. He died and was buried in it in 1065, only a week after it was completed. William I, the Norman conqueror, was crowned there a year later in 1066.

The glorious Gothic style of the building as it stands was set by Henry II in 1220, when he built the Lady Chapel and began rebuilding the original. Over the next five centuries, the Abbey was developed by Henry VII, who continued the Gothic form with his own chapel, and Sir Christopher Wren and his pupil Hawksmoor, who added the twin towers.

There is much to see (and crowds trying to see it all) but the highlights are the tombs and memorials of the many famous people buried, or commemorated, in the Abbey. Among the latter are Chaucer, Shakespeare, and Milton in "poets' corner," as well as many kings and queens of England, the poignant Tomb of the Unknown Warrior, and the Coronation Chair made of oak, used for the coronation of monarchs since the 14th century, and containing the legendary, looted Stone of Scone.

Westminster Abbey is open daily free of charge, except for the Royal Chapels, Poets' Corner, Chapter House of Pyx, and Museum, for which modest charges are made.

The impressive Tate Gallery, Millbank (821–1313), is a 20-minute walk along the Thames going west (or a 77a or 88 bus) in an otherwise uninteresting part of the city. Opened in 1897 specifically as a home for modern British art, it was financed by the sugar broker Henry Tate. The word modern in those days referred to anything post-1790; today the gallery houses many thousands of paintings and sculptures of British and foreign origin from the 16th century to the present. A contentious annex was opened in 1987 to house the hundreds of paintings and drawings that J.M.W. Turner bequeathed to the nation on his death in 1851. The exterior of the new building—in colorful neo-Minoan style—is more attractive than its dreary interior. The Tate has pursued its original aims of being "modern" by exhibiting and purchasing contemporary work that is sometimes controversial. Open Monday to Saturday 10 A.M. to 5:50 P.M., Sunday 2 to 5:50 P.M. Free.

The Tate Gallery is also noted for its basement restaurant (834–6754)—a large room, quite smart, with Rex Whistler's murals on the walls, and service by matronly waitresses. The food is old fashioned British cooking of varied quality and it's best to stick to the straightforward grilled offerings. Of genuine interest, however, is the astonishing range of its wine cellar (call for a copy of the wine list) and the reasonable prices charged—it's worth ordering the most expensive wine you can afford. (Lunch only, Monday through Saturday; no credit cards; reservations advised. About £25 for two.)

Linking Westminster with Trafalgar Square (and completing a round tour if you started out from there to walk to Buckingham Palace) is Parliament Street and Whitehall. This was once the site of the Palace of Whitehall, prosperous home of Cardinal Wolsey, Archbishop of York and Henry VIII's Lord Chancellor in the early 16th century.

Henry VIII took it over in 1529 and under his hand it grew until its buildings and grounds extended over 23 acres. Subsequent monarchs used it, but it was devastated by a fire in the late 17th century and never rebuilt. There are few remnants of the old palace today, with the exception of the magnificent Banqueting House, halfway along Whitehall on the right.

Built in 1622 and commissioned by James I, it represents the introduction of Italian Palladian style into England by the architect Inigo Jones. It would have been used for state banquets, grand court functions, and the like. Rubens painted the ceiling for Charles I who, ironically, 19 years later walked through one of the windows at Banqueting House onto a scaffold to be executed. Open Tuesday to Saturday 10 A.M. to 5 P.M., Sunday 2 to 5 P.M. Admission: 50p.

Whitehall is today lined with government buildings. At its center, the Cenotaph is a simple white monument to Great Britain's war dead. Erected in 1919, it is the scene of an annual wreath-laying ceremony on Remembrance Sunday in November. On the left is Downing Street. No. 10 Downing Street is the official residence of the Prime Minister.

Further along on the left at the Horse Guards stand the mounted guards of the Household Cavalry. Two regiments take turns mounting the guard—the Royal Horse Guards (in blue tunics) and the Life Guards (in scarlet). Through the archway is Horse Guards Parade where, on the Queen's official birthday in June, the ceremonial Trooping of the Colour takes place. The guard is changed daily at 11 A.M. (10 A.M. Sunday) in a half-hour ceremony.

Hyde Park and Kensington Gardens

West of the West End lie Hyde Park and Kensington Gardens—600 acres of grassland, trees, lakes, and wildlife—and the smart residential and shopping areas of Bayswater, Kensington, Knightsbridge, and Belgravia. Until the Industrial Revolution of the 19th century, these were little more than villages surrounded by open fields. But long ago they merged as the urban spread of London engulfed them, yet the various districts retain their individual personalities. Here and there you will even find little pockets with a true village atmosphere. There are many good-value, mid-range hotels here. Some have been converted from Victorian houses, others newly built with all modern comforts. There is also a vast choice of restaurants, pubs, and wine bars.

You could spend a pleasant half-day meandering through Hyde Park's criss-cross paths, exploring its sights and amenities, or just sitting by the Serpentine, a lake. You'll probably want to return for a picnic, or just to relax between shopping and sightseeing trips.

In the days of Henry VIII, Hyde Park was wild countryside, roamed by wolves and deer, with a public gallows, Tyburn, at its northeast corner where two
important Roman roads crossed. The king fancied the
land for hunting deer and game and coerced the owner,
the abbott of Westminster Abbey, into swapping it for
another piece of land further out of town. It remained a
private royal hunting ground for over a century, until it
was opened up by James I for all to enjoy.

Today, near the site of the gallows is Speakers'
Corner, synonymous with free speech. Anyone armed
with a soap box or steps can stand up and speak his mind
on any subject (as long as he doesn't utter obscenities,
profanities, or incite violence); and instead of wolves
there are squirrels and rabbits, a bird sanctuary, and pet
dogs being walked by the score. You can go jogging,
horseback-riding, bike-riding, boating, swimming, or
fishing, or play football, listen to a military or brass band,
have afternoon tea, take a drink or a meal, or just sit in
a deck chair and snooze.

Hyde Park has its own police station—the Royal
Parks Constabulary—and at its southeast corner is the
giant Achilles statue by Richard Westmacott. Paid for by
subscriptions from female fans—who must have had a
collective stroke when the massive nude was unveiled—
cast in bronze and erected in 1822, it honors the Duke
of Wellington, whose former home, Apsley House, at the
entrance to the park at Hyde Park Corner, is now the
Wellington Museum (499–5676).

Wellington was the British general who led the defeat of Napoleon at the battle of Waterloo. The museum
has paintings, works of art, and personal relics of the
Duke. Open Tuesday, Wednesday, Thursday and Saturday 10 A.M. to 6 P.M.; Sunday 2:30 to 6 P.M. Admission
60p.

The enormous traffic island at Hyde Park Corner
also has the triumphal Wellington Arch, a Wellington
statue, and monuments to the Machine Gun Corps and
Royal Artillery.

Along the southern boundary of the park is Rotten
Row, a wide, straight, sandy path for horseback riders
and, since the 19th century, a fashionable place to be

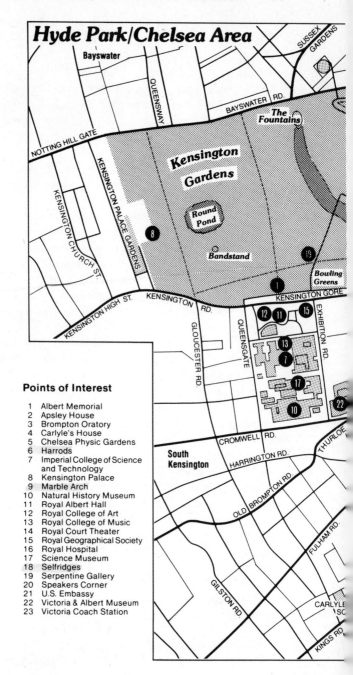

Hyde Park/Chelsea Area

Bayswater

QUEENSWAY

NOTTING HILL GATE

BAYSWATER RD.

The Fountains

Kensington Gardens

KENSINGTON PALACE GARDENS

KENSINGTON CHURCH ST.

Round Pond

8

Bandstand

19

Bowling Greens

KENSINGTON HIGH ST.

KENSINGTON RD.

KENSINGTON GORE

1

KENSINGTON GORE

GLOUCESTER RD.

QUEENSGATE

12   11   15

EXHIBITION RD.

13

7

17

22

10

CROMWELL RD.

South Kensington

HARRINGTON RD.

THURLOE

OLD BROMPTON RD.

FULHAM RD.

GILSTON RD.

CARLYLE SC

KINGS RD.

Points of Interest

1   Albert Memorial
2   Apsley House
3   Brompton Oratory
4   Carlyle's House
5   Chelsea Physic Gardens
6   Harrods
7   Imperial College of Science and Technology
8   Kensington Palace
9   Marble Arch
10 Natural History Museum
11 Royal Albert Hall
12 Royal College of Art
13 Royal College of Music
14 Royal Court Theater
15 Royal Geographical Society
16 Royal Hospital
17 Science Museum
18 Selfridges
19 Serpentine Gallery
20 Speakers Corner
21 U.S. Embassy
22 Victoria & Albert Museum
23 Victoria Coach Station

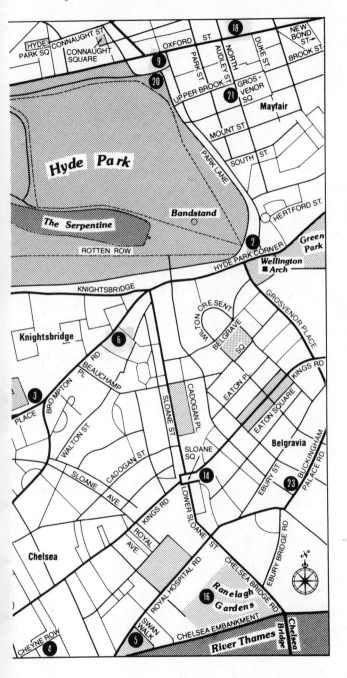

seen riding or driving in one's carriage. The name derives from *route du roi*, French for "the king's way."

The parkland beside Rotten Row was the site of the great International Exhibition of 1851, forerunner of today's world fairs, held in the specially constructed Crystal Palace. The Palace was later transferred to a new site in South London where it was destroyed by fire in 1936.

For refreshments, there is a self-service restaurant/snack bar, The Dell Restaurant, at the eastern-most tip of the Serpentine, and The Serpentine Restaurant, with a more substantial restaurant and bar, near the Serpentine bridge. They can be crowded at the height of the summer, and the food is only passable. Better to bring your own treats and picnic.

North of Hyde Park are the Paddington and Bayswater districts. Paddington has several well-maintained Victorian and Georgian squares, crescents and terraces, notably Connaught Square, Connaught Street, and Hyde Park Square. It is a fashionable residential area favored by foreign embassy diplomats. Paddington's railway terminal is London's rail gateway to the southwest. There is also a canal junction, a vital industrial artery in the early 19th century, now known as "Little Venice." There are many colorful houseboats along the canal, and you can take boat trips from here to the Regents Park Zoo (Zoo Waterbus, 286–6101) and Camden Lock (Jasons Trips, 286–3428).

The Paddington Station area has a number of very cheap hotels and boarding houses, most notably on Sussex Gardens and Norfolk Square.

On the west side of Paddington, and north of Kensington Gardens, is Bayswater, another area of terraces and squares, now largely apartment houses and hotels. On Sundays, the railing along the park on Bayswater Road becomes an open-air art market, drawing strollers and even some buyers. Many of the paintings are chocolate box views of London and thatched cottages, but there is some worthwhile work by genuinely talented artists among the dross.

Le Bistingo, 117 Queensway (727–0743), is one of a chain of cheap and cheerful French brasserie-style restaurants with menus chalked on a blackboard and dripping candles on the tables. Fried mushrooms in tartar sauce, onion soup, and snails are featured among the hors d'oeuvres; fish courses include lemon sole in butter, lemon, and parsley, and trout with almonds; meat dishes include escalope of veal with honey, ham, and cheese; lamb brochette with onions and peppers; and a whole baby chicken grilled and served in a spicy sauce. About £20 for two.

The Standard Indian, 21–23 Westbourne Grove (727–4818), was the first of what are now several Indian restaurants along Westbourne Grove—and one of the most reliable. A large room recently modernized, it is usually full, so make reservations ahead. Appetizers cooked "dry" in the tandoori clay ovens are delicious. Try sheek kebab (minced lamb with onion, herbs, and spices on a skewer) or chicken tikka (chunks of boneless chicken roasted on charcoal). Main courses offer the usual range of "wet" curry dishes, which can be quite mild (butter chicken) or very hot (chicken vindhaloo), or in-between (lamb pasanda—marinated lamb cooked in cream and spices). Around £12 for two.

South of Hyde Park and to the west of Buckingham Palace is Belgravia. Next to Mayfair, it offers London's most fashionable address and contains the elegant Knightsbridge shops with Harrods, several luxury hotels, and a number of fine restaurants.

The proximity of Buckingham Palace led to the development of Belgravia as a residential area for courtiers and to the creation of several magnificent Georgian squares around which many of London's wealthiest folk live—Belgrave and Eaton, as well as the smaller Lowndes, Cadogan, Trevor, Brompton, and Montpelier.

Knightsbridge runs from Hyde Park Corner, parallel

with Hyde Park, as far as the distinctive red brick barracks towers, but it has lent its name to the immediate vicinity. Thus, although Harrods is technically on Brompton Road, which forks away from Knights-bridge at the Scotch House corner, it is widely referred to as a "Knightsbridge store."

To tour the area, start at Hyde Park corner and walk down Knightsbridge. Turn left down Old Barrack Yard and onto Wilton Row, both charming back streets, for **The Grenadier** (see page 118), a historic pub that was once the officers' mess for the Duke of Wellington and which still has its own sentry box.

Back on Knightsbridge take a left at Wilton Place (one of London's exclusive modern hotels, The Berkeley, is on the left) to see Wilton Crescent, Belgrave Square, and, along Belgrave Place, Eaton Square.

Farther along Knightsbridge on the left is the circular Sheraton Park Tower Hotel. Opposite is the rather longer established Hyde Park Hotel, in the grand hotel style, with views over Hyde Park.

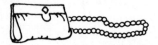

On the next block is **Harvey Nichols,** a department store founded by linen draper Benjamin Harvey in 1813 that specializes in female and male fashions, home furnishings, and household goods.

Off to the right, leading down to Sloane Square and Chelsea, is Sloane Street, the top end of which is solid with fashion boutiques for clothes and shoes, jewelry shops, and home-furnishing shops.

For shoes: **Bally** (9), **Pied à Terre** (14), and **Magli** (207); for ladies' fashions: **Browns** (6c), **Fendi** (37), **Harabel's** (43), and **Courtenay** (188); for jewelry: **Andre Bogaert** (10), **Sloane Pearls** (49), and **Atkinson** (4a).

At the junction with Knightsbridge and Brompton Road is **The Scotch House,** for Scottish tweeds, woolens, cashmere, and, of course, tartans.

Dominating Brompton Road is **Harrods,** one of the world's most famous department stores. Occupying an entire block between Hans Crescent and Hans Road, it is a majestic architectural creation in terracotta brick, as well as a magnificent store. It's difficult to imagine its humble beginnings as a corner grocery back in 1849. The Queen shops here, as do Arab oil sheikhs and many ordinary Londoners and visitors. Despite its "top people's" image, it is not necessarily expensive—unless you're determined to buy a mink coat or gold watch.

Even if you're not in the mood for buying, you must visit Harrods to see, among other things, its legendary food halls, lofty and tiled, and its painstaking set-piece displays of fish and meats. See also its piano department with row upon row of grands and uprights, and its perfume, jewelery, gifts, men's and women's fashion, art gallery, and pet departments.

When you've seen it all, take a drink, and maybe a salad, in Harrods' own pub, The Green Man, down a flight of stairs in the men's tailoring department. This is a cozy, wood-panelled room with comfortable chairs and friendly waitresses to serve you.

On the other side of the street opposite Harrods there's a raised sidewalk and some of London's best (and most expensive) antique shops and galleries: **The Crane Kalman Gallery** (178); **Michael Hogg,** antique furniture (172); **Alistair Sampson,** furniture (156); **John Keil,** furniture (154); and **Earle Vandekar,** plates (138).

St. Quentin, 243 Brompton Road (589–8005), is the ideal place for a relaxing lunch after a hectic morning of shopping. The more-or-less authentic surroundings of a Parisian brasserie offer daily set menus, but a la carte specialties include a fish pâté in green sauce, asparagus in pastry shell, and quail salad for starters; and roasts, grilled meats and fish, and a lobster stew with vegetables for main courses. Finish with chocolate *profiteroles* or the selection of cheeses. Do insist on a table upstairs; the downstairs room is claustrophobic and lacking in atmosphere. About £35 for two.

Even smarter, if that's possible, than Sloane Street and Brompton Road, is Beauchamp Place (pronounced "Beecham"), a narrow, Georgian, terraced sidestreet running off Brompton Road just past Harrods. Every house is now a shop or restaurant, and most of the windows have dazzling displays of the absolute latest in young female fashion, contrasting delightfully with the goods at neighboring antique shops.

For fashions: **Janet Reger,** lingerie (2); **Kanga** (8); **Caroline Charles** (10); **Whistles** (14); **Scruples** (26); and **Bruce Oldfield** (27). For antique silver clocks and guns try **Gage** (1), while the **Map House** (54) is excellent for antique and reproduction maps and prints.

Bill Bentley's, 31 Beauchamp Place (589–5080), is an old established fish restaurant, oyster bar, and wine bar. Packed with "the Knightsbridge set," it is a perfect place for absorbing the local color—if you can stand the noise of upper-class English at its most grating. All sorts of fish cooked in all sorts of ways. About £35 for two.

Walton Street, off to the right from Beauchamp Place, is another elegant, well-prepared terrace. This one features mainly much sought-after town houses, but at the far end there are several excellent restaurants.

Ma Cuisine, 113 Walton Street (584-7585), is a classic French restaurant, generally regarded as one of London's top dining spots. The tiny room (just 11 tables) means that reservations have to be made as far ahead as possible. The short menu changes seasonally, and the many imaginative dishes of the day are described personally to you by Guy Mouilleron the owner-chef.

Among the more unusual starters might be *terrine de poisson aux algues* (fish terrine cooked with seaweed) and *l'oeu vert galant* (a savory tartlet lined with buttered corn, covered by a poached egg and Bearnaise sauce). Fish dishes include mousse of sea-scallop served with a white wine sauce and orange, and trout cooked in butter and served on a bed of fresh tomato with saffron sauce.

Meat courses include leg of chicken stuffed with crabmeat and topped by a lobster sauce and pork filet in a prune and onion cream sauce. It is all, clearly, adventurous stuff—but cooked and served with panache. Expect to pay around £40 for two.

Kensington—part of the Royal Borough of Kensington and Chelsea—is one of London's largest inner boroughs and has many faces. Among them: the royal Kensington Palace, home of Prince Charles and Princess Diana; a road known as "Millionaires' Row"; and, in its northern reaches, a few remaining examples of London's urban decay.

It also has a lot to offer the visitor, including reasonably priced hotels, many well-preserved terraces, squares and houses from the 17th, 18th and 19th centuries; antique shops and general shopping streets; museums of art, science, natural history, and geology; the Royal Albert Hall; the genteel Kensington Gardens; and a wide selection of restaurants.

The area is too widespread to suggest one logical walking tour, so we will simply pinpoint the highlights: South Kensington—bounded by Fulham Road,

Earls Court Road, Kensington High Street, and Exhibition Road—has at its nucleus the area nicknamed by the Victorians "Albertopolis." The museums, galleries, and colleges to the south of the Albert Hall exist thanks to the driving force of Prince Albert, Queen Victoria's husband. It was Albert who promoted the idea of the Great Exhibition of 1851 in Hyde Park and then proposed that the profits be used to purchase the 86 acres now contained by Kensington Gore, Exhibition Road, Queensgate, and Cromwell Road. His idea was to dedicate the area to stimulating popular education and the knowledge of art and science.

He died before the project was completed, but the work was carried out over succeeding decades. The Royal Albert Hall, a magnificent circular building crowned with a great dome, and the Albert Memorial on Kensington Gore, were built as memorials to the man, but the whole area is his legacy, including the Royal College of Art, Royal Geographical Society, Royal College of Organists, Royal College of Music, Royal School of Mines, the Science Museum, Natural History Museum, Victoria and Albert Museum, and the Imperial College of Science and Technology.

The museums, on Cromwell Road and along Exhibition Road, are open from 10 A.M. to 6 P.M. Monday to Saturday; 2:30 P.M. to 6 P.M. Sunday (Victoria and Albert closes at 5:30 P.M.). Admission, when charged, is around £2.50.

The Victoria and Albert (affectionately known as the V & A) houses one of the world's great art collections, with works from virtually all periods and styles.

For dining in the area, the streets around the South Kensington tube station—particularly Old Brompton Road and Thurloe Street—have a good selection of lively, reasonably priced restaurants.

Kensington Gardens, north of Albert Hall, are an extension of Hyde Park, but quieter, with the Round Pond a favorite place for Sunday morning walks, model boat sailing, and kite flying; and the Flower Walk, whose beds are seasonally replanted and gorgeous. On the other side of the broad Walk—the main path through the gardens—is Kensington Palace, home of a number of "royals," including Charles and Di and Princess Margaret. It was the residence of monarchs from 1689 to 1760. The State Apartments can be visited. You can see rooms with furniture and mementos of Queen Victoria and Queen Mary, both of whom were born here, and an interesting museum of court dress. Open Monday to Saturday 9 A.M. to 4:15 P.M., Sunday 1 to 4:15 P.M. Admission: £2.20 (£1 for under 16s).

From the palace, walk through a gate on the left into Kensington Palace Gardens, or "Millionaires' Row." A wide private avenue lined with vast mid-19th-century mansions, it is now occupied almost entirely by foreign embassies.

Winding north from Kensington High Street, by the St. Mary Abbots Church, is Kensington Church Street, a busy thoroughfare leading up to Notting Hill Gate and North Kensington, but an absolute must for antique hunters. Also, the streets around here are fine examples of typical Kensington white stucco Victorian terraces—Palace Gardens Terrace and Brunswick Gardens are especially attractive in the spring, when the cherry trees lining the streets are adorned with pinkish-white blossoms.

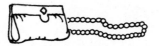

Notable among Kensington Church Street's antique shops are: **Jesse/Laski,** art nouveau and deco (160); **Robert Hales,** swords and military pieces (133); **D. C. Monk,** china and glass (132); **Pamela Teignmouth,** 18th-century furniture (108); **Jonathan Horne,** early English and continental pottery (66c); **Michael German,** arms, armor, walking sticks, wood carvings (38b); **George Horan,** oriental art (38a); and **Pony Express,** art of "the golden West" (U.S. West, that is) (36b).

Geales Fish Restaurant, 2 Farmer Street (727–7969). You've heard all about fish and chips being the staple of the British diet—the original fast food—well, this is the place to sample it. Tucked away on a corner in Hillgate Village at the top of Kensington Church Street, it has a cozy tea-shop appeal and is packed to the gills with locals and discerning visitors. As they don't take reservations, you'll probably have to wait in the small upstairs bar for a table, and you may be asked to share one once they're ready to serve you. But the food is worth waiting for. Start with deep fried clams or home-made fish soup, then choose from the list of fish on the wall menu, likely to include a firm and flaky cod filet, a sweet and juicy plaice, or a vast Dover sole. All will be absolutely fresh and cooked in crisp, golden batter, accompanied by French fries called chips. Drink a bottle of cold Muscadet or champagne to be a little extravagant in the least of extravagant circumstances, and you've had a meal to remember for a mere £15 for two.

Cross Notting Hill Gate at the top of Church Street, then take a right down Pembridge Road, a second left onto Portobello Road, and you're on one of London's best-known market streets. Antique and collector's shops and stalls are at the top, joining a fruit and vegetable market as the road winds downhill. Very few shops are open during the week, and the flea market proper can only be seen on a bustling Saturday. The serious collectors and buyers tend to swoop down early in the day, but you might make a find even in the afternoon.

Monsieur Thompsons, 29 Kensington Park Road
(727–9957), is a North Kensington restaurant to consider for lunch after Portobello Road browsing, or to seek
out for a leisurely dinner. Serious nouvelle French food
is served in a relaxed atmosphere characterized by creak-
ing floorboards, a lofty ceiling, walls covered in sacking
and hung with period mirrors and paintings. The food
looks almost as good as it tastes—the chef believes in
presentation as well as preparation. Scallops in carrot
sauce, brill in lobster sauce, duck in vermouth, and venison in garlic and onions are followed by wonderful desserts including strawberry and basil sorbet. Highly
recommended, but expensive; around £40 for two. Set
menus at £11 and £15 are outstanding value.

Chelsea

Look at a map of London and you'll see that King's Road runs in more or less a straight line from the Buckingham Palace area through Belgravia, Sloane Square, and into Chelsea, linking with other roads leading southwest out of town.

History tells us that this was a path used exclusively by Charles II in the 17th century to visit his mistress, the orange-seller Nell Gwynne; other monarchs used the route to travel to Hampton Court Palace. It became a public thoroughfare only in the early 19th century.

Walk down the Chelsea section of King's Road on a Saturday—from Sloane Square to the kink in the road known as World's End—and you would think that the whole of London now comes to shop, stroll, see, and be seen on this fashion-conscious avenue.

Chelsea used to be a working-class area, but in the 1940s it became popular with actors, writers, and artists, rapidly developing into one of the city's most sought-after, most expensive residential areas. Narrow Victorian terraces have been lovingly restored and prettily decorated. Tiny "bijou" houses now change hands at prices beyond the wildest dreams of their former occupants. In the '50s, Chelsea had a mixed reputation as both Bohemian and dandified; the creative set rubbed shoulders with the socialites and the pubs buzzed with clever conversation. It was a natural place to play host to the denizens of the swinging '60s, with its newfound prosperity, liberalism, and extremes of fashion.

Almost overnight, the old "village" shops along King's Road—the butcher, the greengrocer, the fish seller—disappeared and were transformed into garishly lit, multicolored boutiques or smart restaurants and bistros. King's Road became, and has remained, London's Peacock Alley, although the Nikon-toting foreign press photographers of the '60s, who photographed anything or anybody wearing a miniskirt or dark glasses, have moved on.

It is arguable whether or not Chelsea is the fashion-setter it once was, but King's Road on a Saturday is still a vivid parade, and there are now even more boutiques, wine bars, coffeehouses, and restaurants than ever before. The Saturday scene is enlivened by custom cars cruising the King's Road; in contrast are a number of high-quality antique shops (in the stretch beyond World's End) and antique hypermarkets—something of a supermarket for antiques.

To explore Chelsea, take the tube to Sloane Square (District and Circle lines), a busy traffic island enhanced by attractive gardens and a fountain. The Royal Court Theatre on Sloane Square has long had a reputation for its adventurous policy of encouraging avant-garde playwrights. Early in this century the theater housed the work of G.B. Shaw but perhaps its most famous success of modern times came in 1956 when John Osborne's *Look Back in Anger* was premiered here. Opposite is one of London's best department stores, Peter Jones, noted for home furnishings, china, and glassware. An eminently pleasant place to shop.

The fashion business being what it is, the boutiques along King's Road lead a precarious existence. What is here today could be gone, or have metamorphosed into something completely different, by tomorrow. More likely to be around are the various indoor antique markets—Antiquarius (131–141); Chelsea Antique Market (253);

and Chenil Galleries (181), which specializes in art deco and art nouveau pieces.

To get a flavor of residential Chelsea, take a detour along one of the small streets off King's Road to the right. Or go left onto Royal Avenue, an attractive early- to mid-19th-century terrace that crosses gardens to reach the Royal Hospital. The hospital is one of Chelsea's historical landmarks and home of the famous "Chelsea Pensioners," veteran soldiers who have been cared for there for over 300 years.

The "pensioners," in their scarlet frockcoat summer uniforms, are a startling contrast to the young bucks of the King's Road crowd. The hospital was founded by Charles II and built by Sir Christopher Wren in 1682, and extended in subsequent years. The chapel, Great Hall, and museum can be visited 10 A.M. to noon and 2 to 4 P.M. The garden grounds of the Royal Hospital run down to the river Thames and are the site of the Chelsea Flower Show each May.

Chelsea also has the oldest botanical garden in London, the Chelsea Physic Garden (Swan Walk; 352–5646), founded in 1673 by the Society of Apothecaries. It has an extraordinary history, and only in recent years has it been open to the public. Can you believe, for instance, that the state of Georgia owes its cotton industry to this quiet garden in a secluded backwater of London? It's true. Cotton seeds from the South Seas were nurtured here and sent to Georgia in 1732. Similarly, India's tea passed through here on its way from China, while Malaya's rubber stopped en route from South America. Open 2 to 5 P.M. Wednesday and Sunday, April through October. Admission: £1.50.

The garden is in the Cheyne Walk area of Chelsea, pleasant tree-lined streets of brick terraces, some dating from the 18th century. Here many artists and writers made their homes, among them Turner. At 24 Cheyne Row is the Queen Anne house where the 19th-century Scottish author and historian Thomas Carlyle lived. 19–26 Cheyne Walk is the site of a palace built by Henry VIII that was demolished in the mid-18th century and replaced by the present houses around 1760.

Back on King's Road, the boutiques and restaurants peter out around the World's End district. By now you will likely be ready for a drink at the **World's End Pub,** 459 King's Road—a large, late-Victorian pub, a fine example of its type.

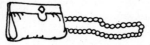

If you are in search of antiques, persevere along the boring area beyond World's End and over the bridge to a less fashionable, but "up and coming" part of King's Road. Known as the Fulham district, there are numerous antique shops about, including **Christopher Wray** (600 King's Road), which has an enormous range of reproductions of Victorian and Edwardian light fixtures.

Wherever you are in Chelsea, you will never be far from somewhere to get a meal. Although the restaurants are perhaps not quite as smart as they were in the '60s, Rolls Royces and Jaguars still sometimes crowd the curb. You'll find everything from award-winning French cuisine to fast-food hamburger joints . . . and most everything in between:

La Tante Claire, 68 Royal Hospital Road (352-6045). Chef Pierre Koffman wins awards and accolades for his cooking at this discreet restaurant in a quiet part of Chelsea near the Embankment. Indeed, one commentator describes him as "the yardstick by which other chefs in this country are judged and judge themselves." The reason for his success is the daring adventurousness of the ingredients he uses, breaking away from traditional

French cooking and even out-shining the best of the nouvelle innovators.

Recently redecorated, the restaurant is larger, more relaxed and far prettier. Leeks with truffles or seafood soup with brandy are among the seven starters. Pigeon or hare with chocolate, rabbit with langoustine, and stuffed pig's feet are among the more creative main courses. For dessert, try meringue with brandy or chocolate filling, and unusual French cheeses.

You can usually reserve a table on relatively short notice at lunch, when the £18.50 set menu represents outstanding value; reservations for dinner, when you could pay around £60 for two, are a must well in advance. Men must wear jacket and tie.

San Frediano, 62 Fulham Road (584-8375). Fulham Road runs parallel to King's Road a block or two north. Near the junction with Sydney Street there is a stretch of smart fashion shops and two or three restaurants, one of which is San Frediano, one of London's most popular places for Italian food.

Two cool rooms are always full and deftly attended by helpful, lively waiters. There's a tempting hors d'oeuvres trolley, and the pasta is homemade. Duck with olives, and grilled langoustines with garlic butter are among the specials. About £30 for two.

Hotels

London has some of the world's most famous traditional grand hotels. Their very names—The Ritz, Savoy, Dorchester, Claridges, Connaught—are synonymous with luxury and style. It isn't necessary to stay at one to get a feel for the degree of service, the ornate decor, and the old-fashioned grace they exude. Amble about their lobbies, stop for a drink, or, in keeping with the English spirit, have afternoon tea on silver service with all the pomp and circumstance you can handle. Even this won't come cheap—about £8 per person for *tea*—but it will be far more economical than staying at these hotels, which cater to expense-account and society clientele. For the record, then, here are the details for the *crème de la crème* of London's hotels. If you choose to pay the price, be assured of super deluxe accommodations in every way. (Our suggestions for more economical, yet still tradition-bound, establishments will follow.) Prices listed throughout this section are for two people sharing a twin or double room and include VAT (Value Added Tax) and service unless otherwise indicated.

Berkeley, Wilton Pl., SW1X 7RL (235-6000) £165–

180.

Claridges, Brook St., W1A 2JQ (629-8860); £170–195.

Connaught, Carlos Place, W1Y 6AL (499-7070); £132–155 plus 15% service.

Dorchester, Park Lane, W1A 2HG (629-8888); £191.

Ritz, Piccadilly, W1V 9DG (493-8181); £160.

Savoy, Strand, WC2R OEU (836-4343); £150–210.

The tourist industry boom of the past 20 years has also brought a rash of new hotels. Many are part of uniform international chains catering to tourist and business groups. Some, notably the Inn on the Park, Hamilton Place, W1 1AZ (499-0888), £170 plus VAT, and the Inter-Continental, 1 Hamilton Place, W1V OQY (409-3131), £191, provide gracious living in the style of the grand hotels but with ultramodern facilities.

At the other end of the scale are innumerable small hotels offering bed and breakfast, with probably only a washbasin in the room, or maybe a shower, and a bathroom shared with other guests. The quality of these budget places varies enormously, but you can be assured of cleanliness and courtesy if you pick one registered with the British Tourist Authority (check at Tourist Information, 26 Grosvenor Gardens, SW1W ODU, 730-3488). In the U.S., contact the British Tourist Authority, 40 W. 57th Street, Third Floor, New York, NY 10019 (212-581-4700). Bed and breakfast hotels and guesthouses typically cost £25–35 per room.

If you arrive in London without reserved accommodations (not recommended at the height of the summer season), London Tourist Board information centers at Heathrow Airport and Victoria Station will help you find a room.

Special rates for weekends can sometimes be found —especially off-season. Check for availability when reserving or via your travel agent. Also, many airlines offer package deals that include airfare and room at considerable savings, though the lodgings are usually at the large tourist hotels. Again, best to check with a travel agent.

The hotels we recommend below fall between the

super deluxe and the bed and breakfast in price, accommodation, and service. They have some character and atmosphere while providing most, if not all, modern comforts; don't expect air conditioning—by and large England's climate doesn't warrant it.

BAYSWATER

Whites Hotel, 90 Lancaster Gate, W2 3NR (262-2711). Whites' appropriately whitewashed, porticoed Edwardian frontage on Bayswater Road is beside Hyde Park and Kensington Gardens. It is a well established hotel in the old-fashioned style, but comfortably furnished and modernized over the years. Rooms have modern facilities, including mini-bar refrigerators. Only a few minutes walk from Marble Arch and the West End, and ideally placed for early morning joggers. From £120; service is optional.

BELGRAVIA/VICTORIA

Ebury Court, 26 Ebury Street, SW1W OLU (730-8147). A conversion of several terraced houses, this personally run hotel also provides a taste of the English way of life at reasonable prices. Rooms without bath are £57, with bath £67—gratuities not included, but with English breakfast. Near Victoria Station.

Goring Hotel, Beeston Place, Grosvenor Gardens SW1W 0JW (834-8211). Founded by O. R. Goring in 1910 and now run by his grandson, the Goring is something of a rarity in the hotel world—a top-class establishment owned and personally supervised by one family independent of any chain or corporation. They claim it was the first hotel in the world to be equipped with a bathroom and central heating in every bedroom, and the present owner/manager George Goring says he has slept in every bedroom himself "in order to ensure that they are as comfortable as they look." Elegantly furnished and decorated, close to Buckingham Palace, and with its own private gardens, the Goring boasts a high staff-to-bedroom ratio and "three lady housekeepers who are absolute perfectionists." Highly recommended. From £115.

Wilbraham Hotel, 1 Wilbraham Place, Sloane Street, SW1X 9AE (730–8296). On a quiet side street just north of Sloane Square and within easy reach of Knightsbridge is this well-kept and comfortable hotel. It has been described as a typical English country inn transplanted to the heart of the city. Double £48, excluding VAT and service.

KENSINGTON

Kensington Close Hotel, Wrights Lane, W8 5SP (937-8170). This is one of the few multiroom hotels we recommend, selected for its excellent value, its position in the heart of Kensington, and the wide range of its facilities. The 530 bedrooms are comfortable if unexceptional, and there is a cocktail bar and two restaurants. But it's the recreational facilities that make this hotel stand out in its class—indoor pool, two ventilated squash courts, saunas, solarium, and fully-equipped gymnasium. From £62.

Blakes Hotel, 33 Roland Gardens, SW7 3PF (370-6701). Among the most fashionable of London's small hotels, this Victorian terraced house was converted to a hotel by owner/interior designer Anouska Hempel. Convenient to the South Kensington museums and Knightsbridge shopping, it features 48 individually decorated suites and rooms. Stylish decor and stylish clientele from the world of gossip columns, show business, and fashion. Also renowned for its restaurant. From £145.

Number Sixteen, 16 Sumner Place, SW7 3EG (589-5232). Yet another conversion of a mid-19th-century terraced house (actually houses, because it also encompasses Nos. 15 and 17) offering personal service and a townhouse ambience. From £70–85. Light breakfast included; service extra.

Portobello Hotel, 22 Stanley Gardens, W11 2NG (727-2777). Another personally run, highly individual small hotel, converted from a Victorian, terraced house close to antique shops and stalls at the top end of Portobello Road. This is a colorful, bustling area of Kensington, near Notting Hill Gate tube station and within walking distance of Kensington Gardens. The hotel looks onto its own pleasant gardens. The bedrooms, some of which are quite small, are furnished and decorated to a high standard. Doubles are £67, "special" rooms, some with four-poster beds, about £78, excluding service.

Gore Hotel, 189 Queen's Gate, SW7 5EX (584-6601). A friendly atmosphere, heightened by personal touches—with some typically English decor, an oak-beamed Tudor Room, linenfold paneling, a minstrels' gallery, even a fourposter bed; the Venus Room is in ornate Italian style. 54 rooms, 5 suites, and close to the Royal Albert Hall and Kensington Gardens. From £75.

KNIGHTSBRIDGE/CHELSEA

11 Cadogan Gardens, Sloane Square, SW3 2RJ (730-3426). This large Victorian terraced house, typical of this area of Chelsea near the Sloane Square end of King's Road was converted and furnished with the aim of preserving its character. A solid, discreet hotel favored by diplomats and discerning tourists. From £94 to £124.

Knightsbridge Green Hotel, 159 Knightsbridge SW1X 7PD (584-6274). Right in the heart of the Knightsbridge shopping area, this hotel offers a homey atmosphere, personal service, and excellent value at £60; VAT extra. No bar or restaurant.

Capital Hotel, Basil Street, SW3 1AT (589-5171). One of two top class hotels on Basil Street, lying just a credit-card throw from Harrods department store. Luxuriously fitted with leather, wood, and deep pile carpets.

Bathrooms come with robes, toothbrushes, razors, etc. Particularly good restaurant. From £135.

Basil Street I Hotel, Knightsbridge, SW3 1AH (581-3311). An elegant, old-fashioned, medium-sized hotel with lots of antique furniture and good old-fashioned service. Built as a hotel in 1910 and privately operated along the lines of a country house hotel. There is a spacious lounge for cocktails or afternoon tea, a formal dining room, an informal buffet, and also a wine bar. From £94.

Hyde Park Hotel, 66 Knightsbridge, SW1 7LA (235-2000). A pride of the vast Trust House Forte chain, this is a magnificent survival from more elegant days. If you can't afford to stay here, at least drop by the marble and silk interior for lunch or tea overlooking the park. Opulent, pricey, and a classic. From £160.

COVENT GARDEN/STRAND

Drury Lane Hotel, 10 Drury Lane, WC2B 5RE (836-6666). A large, modern hotel ideally situated for the restaurants and shops of Covent Garden and the theaters of Shaftesbury Avenue. Attractive lobby area with a cool, green-garden atmosphere created by lots of plants and green decor. Maudie's Restaurant enables you to fill up on a first course before the theater and return for main course and dessert afterwards. From £99. No service charge.

Strand Palace Hotel, Strand,, WC2R OJJ (836-8080). A no-fuss, no-frills, giant across the street from the famous Savoy. Excellently sited for shopping in the Covent Garden complex, for theatergoing, or just enjoying the town. Another Trust House Forte hotel. From £66–75.

Waldorf Hotel, Aldwych, WC2B 4DD (836-2400). Large traditional hotel dominating the Aldwych between Strand and Fleet Streets, well placed for Covent Garden. Edwardian period decor and furnishings throughout and particularly splendid Palm Court for afternoon tea or drinks. From £100.

WEST END

Brown's Hotel, Albermarle Street, W1A 4SW (493-6020). Founded by James Brown, a former butler to Lord Byron, Brown's has retained its Victorian period atmosphere and is favored by many visitors who want modern facilities in a traditional hotel setting. Wood panelling, extensive carpeting, and antique furniture all lend to the overall feeling of a Victorian club. Bedrooms are charming. The L'aperitif restaurant serves traditional and new French cuisine. From £135–£160.

Britannia, Grosvenor Square, W1A 3AN (629-9400). Close to the American Embassy, the Britannia is a 435-room hotel maintained in keeping with the Georgian history of Grosvenor Square. It has its own bow-fronted interior shopping arcade. Luxurious rooms have all facilities, and there's a French restaurant, cocktail bar, pub, coffee shop, and Japanese restaurant. From £130 plus VAT.

Chesterfield Hotel, 34-36 Charles Street, W1X 8LX (491-2622). Just off Berkeley Square near Shepherd Market, the Chesterfield stands on the site where the Earls of Chesterfield had their London home. It has 85 rooms but the feel of a much smaller hotel, and manages to combine elegance with friendly charm. There's self-service buffet dining and a restaurant in Regency style. From £115, excluding service.

Durrants Hotel, George Street, W1H 6BJ (935-8131). An historic London hotel dating back to the late 18th century and for many years popular with English people visiting London from "the country." Modern comforts and facilities with charming decor. Situated close to the Wallace Collection museum in the Marylebone district. From £70.

Flemings Hotel, 10 Half Moon St., W1Y 7RA (499-2964). Attractive period hotel, with plenty of Between-the-Wars atmosphere. Recently redecorated, with a good restaurant and pleasant staff. Sited just off Piccadilly, and so very handy indeed for the avid shopper and theater maven. From £90.

Royal Trafalgar Thistle, Whitcombe St., WC2H 7HG (930-4477). Conveniently sited right behind the National Gallery—and so in the center of sightseeing London. Part of a reliable chain, with other hotels scattered around the West End. A medium size hotel with efficient staff. From £92.

Shopping

As befits one of the great trading capitals of the world, London's shops are able to boast the slogan: "You name it, we sell it." Finding "it" and buying "it" can be an abominable experience (Oxford Street on a Saturday morning), or a delight (Camden Lock craft shops on a summer Sunday morning). You can pamper yourself in the luxury of Harrods or Bond Street's designer stores, or you can stroll the colorful street markets at Petticoat Lane. You can explore Covent Garden or search for an antique bargain along Portobello Road.

Most West End shops open at 9 or 9:30 A.M. and close at 5:30 P.M., and many shops in the West End, especially the department stores and fashion boutiques, stay open until 7:30 P.M. on Thursday (Wednesday for some Knightsbridge shops).

Credit cards are widely accepted, traveler's checks less so, and some of the larger shops operate a scheme which waives the 15 per cent VAT (value added tax) for overseas visitors. You need to show your passport and fill out a form at the time of purchase.

Exactly what you buy to take home, for yourself or as gifts, depends largely on your budget and your taste.

London can offer a very wide choice in handcrafted items
—pottery, carved wood and bone, silver, semi-precious
stones—they need only seeking out. You will still find
plenty of British-made cashmere pullovers, tweed jackets, Scottish woolens, and some traditionally styled shoes
that are good value.

As a very rough guide, Oxford Street has the moderately priced department stores and cheaper clothes
shops; Bond Street and Regent Street have the more
expensive clothes shops and jewelry shops; there's more
fashion, at the middle and top price ranges, around
Knightsbridge. Jermyn Street has the men's shirt and
shoe shops. Covent Garden has just about everything
(but watch the prices—they are creeping up as its reputation as a tourist draw grows). For top-class antiques go
to Bond Street, Knightsbridge, and Kensington; for
cheaper antiques and bric-a-brac try the hypermarkets in
Chelsea and the stalls in Portobello Road and Camden.
Art galleries abound on and around Bond Street.

Finding presents for the folks back home can be the
biggest headache on vacation trips. If you want something that is guaranteed to be Made In England, try the
Design Centre Shop (28 Haymarket, near Piccadilly Circus), which houses a permanent exhibition of the latest
and best of British designs. All merchandise at the Centre is for sale.

For men, why not take home one of those items of
clothing that epitomize the London city businessman or
the archetypal Englishman—the "black derby" bowler
hat? Buy one from the shop that made the first bowler,
the 200-years-old **James Lock** (6 St. James's Street).
They call it a Coke hat, which has nothing to do with the
drink, but was the name of the man they made it for.

If you're buying one for yourself, they'll measure
your head with a special Victorian device and mold the
hat to your head's shape. You could buy one just to hang
on the wall—but don't tell the Lock's salesman.

For other unusual gift ideas: **Strangeways,** 4 North-
ington Street, in Holborn, a cooperative workshop specializing in handpainted china; **The Tea House,** 15a Neal
Street, for teas, teapots, and tea-making accessories; **The**

Kite Store, 69 Neal Street, for kites in original designs; **Smythsons,** 54 New Bond Street, for stationery as supplied to Buckingham Palace; **General Trading Company,** 144 Sloane Street, for a smart bazaar-type shop stocking a wide variety of useful and useless things.

The designer-name shops for women's fashions are in Knightsbridge, Sloane Street, and Bond Street. Also worthwhile: **Liberty's,** 214-222 Regent Street, especially for their own prints; **Jaeger,** 200-206 Regent Street, for well-cut, subtle colors; **Laura Ashley,** 208 Regent Street and also in Covent Garden, for original designs and reasonable prices; **Fenwick,** 63 New Bond Street—for a wide range of accessories at good prices; **Browns,** 27 South Molton Street, for top-class designs from the continent; **Whistles,** 14 Beauchamp Place, featuring the best of British collections; **Zandra Rhodes,** 14a Grafton Street, the shop of a famous British designer noted for beautiful, expensive, and controversial dresses.

For well-made, traditional, and (subdued) contemporary men's clothes, in descending order of price range: **Aquascutum,** 100 Regent Street; **Harrods,** Knightsbridge; **Simpson's,** Piccadilly; **Austin Reed,** 103 Regent Street. For men's shirts, try **Turnbull & Asser,** 71 Jermyn Street; **Harvie & Hudson,** 77 Jermyn Street; **Hilditch & Key,** 37 and 73 Jermyn Street; **Gieves & Hawkes,** 1 Savile Row. For shoes: **Trickers,** 67 Jermyn Street; **John Lobb,** 9 St. James's Street.

Shops with more fashionable clothes for men include **Browns,** 27 South Molton Street, which is first class, expensive, and worth it; **Tommy Nutter,** 19 Savile Row, which tailors to show-business clientele but also sells ready-made merchandise; also various boutiques around Covent Garden and along King's Road and Beauchamp Place.

Jewelers are spread out all over town. Among the finest are **Asprey's,** 165-169 New Bond Street, an old, established shop patronized by London society for decades and good for gift ideas; **Cartier,** 175 New Bond Street, surely one of the world's most famous names;

Garrard, 112 Regent Street, with jewelry by appointment to the Royal Family. Silver items can be found at **The Silver Vaults,** Chancery House, Chancery Lane, with underground vaults stocked with antique and new silver.

London has so many antique shops selling such a wide variety of wondrous items that it is almost impossible to select individual shops for mention in this brief section. However, most shoppers for antiques are first and foremost browsers, and what we can do is suggest areas to explore: Knightsbridge/Brompton Road, Beauchamp Place, King's Road, and New King's Road, Fulham Road, Kensington Church Street, Old and New Bond Street, Covent Garden Piazza, Portobello Road, Camden Passage, and Bermondsey Market. Also the auction rooms: **Christies,** 8 King Street (839-9060); **Bonhams,** Montpelier Street (584-9161); **Phillips,** 7 Blenheim Street (629-6602); **Sotheby's,** 34-35 New Bond Street (493-8080).

A wide variety of handmade craft goods can be found at **Contemporary Applied Arts,** 43 Earlham Street; **The Coppershop,** 48 Neal Street; **Craftsmen Potters Shop,** Marshall Street; **Naturally British,** 13 New Row (clothes, toys, furniture, gifts in a fascinating little shop); **Scottish Merchant,** 16 New Row, for Scots-made knitwear; **The Glasshouse,** 65 Long Acre.

The Charing Cross Road area has enough bookshops to keep even the most dedicated bookworm busy for days. **Foyle's,** 199 Charing Cross Road, is in an old, overcrowded building, with many floors and a maddening maze of a layout. Shopping here is not a pleasure, but there's a lot of choice.

Waterstone's, 121 Charing Cross Road, is one of a new chain with an up-to-date stock of books ranging over a wide variety of subjects—it's very good in travel. Charing Cross Road also has several shops selling overstocks at bargain prices, as well as secondhand and special-interest shops—Cecil Court, off the south end, just above Trafalgar Square, is lined with them.

Hatchards, 187 Piccadilly, is said to be London's oldest bookshop, good for modern fiction, travel, and paperbacks. **Dillons University Bookshop,** 1 Malet Street, serves the nearby college campus, and so is good on scholarly books, but also excellent across the general range of interests.

The book department at **Harrods** is suitably impressive, with a vast section of paperbacks. Other department stores—**Liberty** (Regent Street), **Harvey Nichols** (Knightsbridge), and **Selfridges** (Oxford Street) also have good book departments.

Penhaligon's, 41 Wellington Street, WC2, uses old-time formulae to make their own perfumes and soaps for men and women. **Floris,** 89 Jermyn Street, and **Harrods'** perfume department are good for these items as well.

Art galleries are largely centered around Bond Street and its immediate surroundings. Among the best known: **Wildenstein,** 147 New Bond Street, is an internationally famous dealer in Old Masters; **Browse & Darby,** 19 Cork Street, offers paintings and sculpture; **Marlborough Fine Art,** 6 Albermarle Street, specializes in contemporary graphics. For fun, and maybe for something that will catch your eye, browse the open-air art markets along the railings on the Green Park side of Piccadilly and the Hyde Park side of Bayswater Road on Sundays.

Housewares are available at **Heals/Habitat,** 196 Tottenham Court Road; **Divertimenti,** 68 Marylebone Lane, for excellent, mainly French-made, kitchenware; **David Mellor,** 4 Sloane Square, and 26 James Street WC2, for plain and mainly modern ware, and good British pottery.

Petticoat Lane (actually on the map as Middlesex Street, opposite Liverpool Street Station) has a Sunday morning, East End market filled with lots of fun junk and a lively scene. If you think you speak English, try to understand what the fast-talking market traders are saying in their sales spiels.

Camden Passage, Islington High Street, is another open market good for bric-a-brac and antiques. There are also several restaurants here, topped by Frederick's. Best to go on Saturday mornings, but shops are open all week and stalls on Tuesday, Wednesday, and Saturday mornings.

Camden Lock (at Chalk Farm Road and Regents Canal—take the tube to Camden Town, or canal boat from Little Venice; 286-3428). Flea market stalls with potentially interesting junk and antiques abound, as well as craft shops in converted warehouses by the lock.

Portobello Road, W11 (Notting Hill Gate tube), has numerous shops and stalls along a winding, downhill lane. The traders are good-humored and you may even find a bargain, but start early to beat the serious collectors. Peters out into a lively fruit and vegetable market. Most of the shops open only on Saturday.

Culture

London's array of cultural entertainment is as colorful, diverse, tempting, and confusing as a dessert trolley in a top-class French restaurant. Whether it be opera, ballet, classical music in all its forms, drama, comedy, or musicals, you'll find it, any night, somewhere in London. The choice is yours.

To help you make the choice, consult the weekly listings magazine *Time Out* which is as close to comprehensive as can be, although its young staff leans heavily towards the alternative society view of things. *The Times* and *The Independent* have good arts listings, with the latter, a newcomer in the field, carrying the best coverage.

There are 40 or more theaters in the West End, clustered around Shaftesbury Avenue and Covent Garden. Dozens more fringe theaters are in pubs and small halls. There are three major opera and ballet houses, seven major concert halls, and two subsidized arts centers for music and drama. Important note: orchestra seats, as they are known in the United States, are called stalls (sometimes orchestra stalls) in England; boxes are the same as in the United States, while mezzanine or first tier are called dress circle; and balcony is upper circle.

London is one of the world's great centers for theater, its dramatic exports in particular lighting up the Great White Way in New York, and its Shakespearean productions unparalleled anywhere in the world. As such, there is no accepted theater season in London, although producers aim to establish their hoped-for box office successes in time for the main summer tourist season. You can purchase tickets in person at the theaters, or reserve by telephone and collect your seats no later than half an hour before curtain. Alternatively, you can buy tickets by phone, charging them to your credit card and picking them up at the last minute. Curtain times vary as do the days matinees are given (no drama performances are given on Sundays), and tickets seldom list the time of the performance—so ask when you purchase them or check the daily papers.

The most economical way of going to the theater is to use the half-price ticket booth on Leicester Square, open from noon to 2 P.M. for matinees and from 2:30 to 6:30 P.M. for evening performances. It offers unsold tickets on the day of the performance only; you get no choice of location (but they are best available seats) and you have to pay cash. All tickets are half-price plus a 75p service charge. One person may buy no more than four tickets. The line forms about 1:45 P.M. for evening performances; the longest wait is about 45 minutes. Something is always to be had even at 6:30 P.M.

Unless the show you want is completely sold out, it won't be necessary to use the ticket agencies. Some add a surcharge despite the likelihood that the theater box office itself is only a few minute's walk away—sometimes even right next door. Sometimes agencies can help when it's standing room only, but blockbuster sell-outs are few and far between. If you are concerned about seeing a particular show, you can order seats before you leave the U.S. from Edwards and Edwards, One Times Square, New York, NY 10036 (212-944-0290), or from Keith Prowse, 234 West 44th Street, New York, NY 10036 (212-398-1430 or 800-223-4446).

Top-price West End theater seats are about £15, which Londoners think expensive, though a bargain compared to Broadway. Programs are not free, as in the

States, though; you purchase them from the ushers or the people selling snacks and soft drinks. As on Broadway, though, theater bars are small, under-staffed, and over-priced. You can order an intermission drink before the first act curtain—or pop out quickly to the nearest pub.

If you want an intriguing night at the theater, try one of the fringe companies, the London equivalent of Off—or even Off Off—Broadway. For information search through *Time Out,* or contact the Fringe Theater Box Office, Duke of York's Theater, St. Martin's Lane, WC2 (379 6002). The helpful staff will also answer queries from abroad.

Opera and ballet-lovers are catered to by the **Royal Opera House** in Covent Garden (the box office is on Floral Street, around the corner from the main entrance; 240-1066), the **London Coliseum** (St. Martin's Lane; 836-3161), and the **Sadlers Wells Theatre** (Roseberry Avenue, 278-8916).

The Royal Opera House is the home of the Royal Ballet Company as well as the Royal Opera Company. The main opera season starts around September 1. Top-price tickets are fixed at £40, though as we go to press a top price of £75 is threatened. There is a fair percentage of seats at a much lower price. Tickets always sell out quickly, so try to reserve before leaving the U.S.

The London Coliseum is the home of the English National Opera which, as its name suggests, performs English-language translations of an extensive range of operas, and has some of the most exciting and avant garde opera productions to be seen anywhere in the world. Its prices are less than a third of the Garden ones, and excellent value. The London Festival Ballet company also appears here during the summer.

Sadlers Wells is host to visiting companies as well as its own in-house opera troupe, and also to some ballet and contemporary dance performances.

The major concert halls are the **Royal Festival Hall, Queen Elizabeth Hall,** and **The Purcell Room** (928-3191), all at the South Bank Arts complex; **The Royal Albert Hall** (589-8212) on Kensington Gore alongside Hyde Park; **Barbican Hall** (628-8795), in the arts center in the City Barbican complex; **Wigmore Hall** (935-2141) on Wigmore Street; and **St. John's,** Smith Square (222-1061), a deconsecrated church.

All are interesting venues in their own right, but if you have to choose, try and see something at the Royal Albert Hall. The rows of terraced seats and red plush and gilt boxes and the vast organ dominating the stage in the circular interior are even more stunning than the exterior view of this extraordinary building.

From July to September the Royal Albert Hall features the BBC's Promenade concerts, with orchestra seats removed and the central floor area filled with promenaders; who bring an air of fun and excitement to what might otherwise be solemn occasions. In the summer check for open-air concerts in London's many parks (633-1707).

The Barbican, opened in 1982, is home of the Royal Shakespeare Company, the London Symphony Orchestra, and the English Chamber Orchestra. There is one of the world's most excitingly designed theaters, a concert hall, a "pit" theater for new and experimental drama, a movie house, an art gallery, and restaurants.

The **National Theatre** on the South Bank (Upper Ground; 928-2252) has three theaters—the Olivier, Lyttelton, and Cottesloe. The Olivier is, of course, named after Lord (Laurence) Olivier, who was also the National Theatre Company's first director. It was opened in 1976 amid controversy over its stark concrete exterior.

Restaurants

Luckily for the visitor who likes food, the eating habits of the British have changed dramatically over the last few years. Once upon a time, London presented a most unadventurous choice of restaurants, but a combination of immigration from Europe and the Far East, widespread foreign travel by the British themselves, more disposable income; and larger expense accounts, has created a fascinating new pattern to dining out.

From *nouvelle cuisine* or *cuisine minceur,* which the British suspect of being a French con trick—less on the plate, more on the check—to Chinese delicacies, American deep-dish pizzas, raw Japanese subtleties, brain-blowing Indian curries, even rediscovered English classics like beef-and-oyster pie, the whole world of international food can be explored on the tables of London's restaurants.

The trouble is that exploring can come expensive. When compared with European or American restaurants, London's are definitely pricey. Finding a good inexpensive meal is a thankless task, though ethnic restaurants tend to be shining exceptions to the rule. When not eating out on expense accounts, Londoners head for neighborhood Indian, Chinese, or Greek places.

Generally speaking, the most interesting restaurants, and some of the oldest, are clustered around Soho, Bayswater, Kensington, and Chelsea. Most have menus in their windows, so you can get an idea of specific offerings and prices. However, be careful about cover charges, Value Added Tax (VAT), and service charges.

Fifteen percent VAT is supposed to be included in the prices on the menu, but some restaurants add it on to the final bill instead. Service charges of 10-15 percent are usually added automatically to the food and beverage subtotal, but some restaurants have the unfortunate habit of adding it to the bill and then presenting you with a credit card voucher with the tip space left empty (despite its inclusion on the regular bill), hoping you'll add it again. Don't. Tip beyond the service charge if you wish, but it's not generally expected.

For that one *very* special meal—at a price—consider La Tante Claire, Le Gavroche, and Simply Nico. For the liveliest ambience, try Langan's Brasserie, the Chicago Pizza Pie Factory, Jams, Joe Allen, and the Hard Rock Cafe. Each is described in greater detail below.

The majority of restaurants these days have interesting wines from all over the world, though most are from Europe. Wine by the glass is usually limited to one red and one white house wine, though wine bars sell a much wider selection that way. House wine by the bottle or carafe is the best bet for the budget conscious, as wine prices in London tend to be distinctly on the high side.

In 1987 a long overdue change to English licensing laws enabled restaurants to serve alcohol with meals during the once dry hours between 3 and 5:30 P.M. Not every restaurant takes advantage of the new law, but many have extended their lunch hours. As a general guideline, any place calling itself a Brasserie or Cafe will serve hot meals and alcohol throughout the afternoon.

There aren't many restaurants where you can eat after 11:30 although you won't find it a problem getting a meal immediately after the theater as long as you don't dally on the way to the restaurant. Most last orders must be placed between 11 and 11:30 P.M. Some exceptions are Lou Pescadou, Joe Allen, and Café Pelican.

For a quick lunchtime snack while sightseeing or shopping, stop in at one of the many sandwich bars. They are usually clean, friendly, and good value for the money —but don't expect an American-style sandwich. The English sandwich (and it was, after all, an Englishman, Lord Sandwich, who created the idea) comprises two thin slices of white or wheat bread with a single filling plus, perhaps, lettuce or tomato.

England is also justly famous for what many might consider a fourth daily meal: afternoon tea. Most of the grand hotels serve it in their lobbies between 4 and 6 P.M. You can fill up on delicately cut cucumber sandwiches, scones, and cream cakes, with a pot of tea as only the English brew it. It's a very civilized way of passing an hour after shopping and sightseeing or before the theater, and just substantial enough to hold you until a late dinner.

ENGLISH

The English House, 3 Milner Street, SW3 (584-3002); **The English Garden,** 10 Lincoln Street, SW3 (584-7272); and **Lindsay House,** 21 Romilly Street, W1 (439-0450). These are sister restaurants in Chelsea, the first with a main Victorian-style dining room and private facilities upstairs, the second a domed and white-washed conservatory. All get high marks for food based on old English recipes. Appetizers include asparagus cream tart, smoked salmon with horseradish sauce, and "scarlet Windsor salad"—sticks of seasonal red vegetables with red Windsor cheese tossed in a light strawberry vinegar dressing. Main course suggestions: roast lamb with cheese and almonds and braised duck stuffed with mixed fruit, spices, and nuts, served with a ginger, apricot, and rum sauce. £37 for two will include dessert or cheese.

Porters, 17 Henrietta Street, WC2 (379-3556). This split-level restaurant is convenient to Covent Garden, its name deriving from the old market porters. The specialties here are pies with a variety of fillings—steak, oyster, and clam; chicken and sweet corn; lamb and apricot; turkey and chestnut, etc. All are said to be "traditional homemade," though there aren't too many English homes eating steak with oysters and clams. They *are* consistently delicious, and a good value at £3 each. Add a salad, dessert, wine, and coffee and the bill will run about £8 per person.

Rules, 35 Maiden Lane, WC2 (836-5314). Said to be London's oldest restaurant, Rules dates back to 1798. The atmosphere is solidly Edwardian, with memories of Lily Langtry, Edward VII's mistress. Stick with simply prepared omelettes, fish, grilled meats, poultry, and pies. Daily specials can include roast venison and red cabbage, boiled beef with carrots and dumplings, grouse, and steak and kidney pie. Take a hearty appetite and about £40 for two.

Tate Gallery, *see* page 64.

AMERICAN

Hard Rock Cafe, *see* page 55.

Jams, 42 Albermarle Street, W1 (493-3600). A Mayfair branch of the New York restaurant that was the first to bring Californian cuisine to London. Stylish and expensive. Fish and chicken are marinated, chargrilled, and served with fashionable "art on the plate" vegetables. Superb American desserts. Pricey French and Californian wine list. Three courses with wine for two can cost £50–£70, including tip and cover.

Joe Allen, *see* page 33.

CHINESE

Dumpling Inn, 15a Gerrard Street, W1 (437-2567). Nothing like an inn—just two small rooms (don't let them seat you downstairs) on a corner of London's Chinatown just a stroll from the theaters on Shaftesbury Ave. A favorite for return visits. Try the deep-fried seaweed with dried scallops, half a dozen steamed dumplings, shredded beef in chili, and chicken in yellow bean sauce. A feast for two will run £15.

Ken Lo's Memories of China, 67-69 Ebury Street, SW1 (730-7734). Who is Ken Lo and what is he remembering? Mr. Lo is Britain's acknowledged authority on Chinese cuisine. He writes about it, lectures about it, makes video cassettes about it, and runs the Chinese Gourmet Club. His memories are of great Chinese meals. His restaurant, on a residential street near Victoria Station, is luxurious and spacious, with wood screens creating semi-private dining areas. Lo's kitchen turns out dishes from different regions, so his menu changes every few months. Don't be afraid to ask for help in sorting out the large menu, or choose one of the set £8-£16 meals. If you're ordering a la carte, be sure to include spring rolls and sesame shrimp toast for starters, and chicken in ginger or seafood in black bean sauce as a main course.

Poon's, 41 King Street, WC2 (240-1743). There are two other Poon's; on Lisle Street and Leicester Street; but this Covent Garden outlet is the flagship. The glass-walled kitchen is in the center of the restaurant, with tables grouped around it in a horseshoe so you can watch the chefs preparing your food in spotlessly clean surroundings. Poon's is famous for wind-dried meats such as Lap Yuck Soom—finely chopped bacon stir fried with bamboo shoots and water chestnuts, served with lettuce. And that's just a starter. For main courses, try Buddha's Hand Chicken or Three-Course Duck Kiam Ling, which utilizes the duck's crispy skin, bone (for soup), and the meat. About £30 for two.

Tai Pan, 8 Egerton Gardens Mews, SW3 (589–

8287). Another elegant Chinese restaurant, this one in a large basement decorated in colonial style. Ideal for parties as the chef will prepare a special menu; the food is mostly Pekinese, with hot and spicy Szechuan dishes, too. This is a fashionable spot much favored by London Society—the Queen's photographer-cousin, Lord Lichfield, is the owner! An average bill for two with wine will be £40.

FRENCH

Le Gavroche, see page 50.

Grill St. Quentin, 136 Brompton Road, SW3 (581–8377). Relative of the elegant St. Quentin restaurant opposite, this Grill is also straight out of Paris, though this is a sophisticated fast food operation. Fish and meat are chargrilled and served with excellent *pommes frites;* cheese comes, via the company's delicatessen, from doyen Philippe Olivier in Boulogne. Authentic bread and patisseries are made in the St. Quentin. Open from midday until midnight every day. Reckon on £15 a head for two courses and wine.

Langan's Brasserie, *see* page 54.

Lou Pescadou, 241 Old Brompton Road, SW5 (370 –1057). A useful place to remember if you have to eat in Earls Court. Run by the South of France team who own the fish restaurants La Croisette and Le Suquet, this is an up-to-date bistro where the specialty is fish. Hence oysters, mussels, clams and other shellfish are available individually or part of a plateau de fruits de mer. Also on the menu are French pizza, ravioli with crab, and plainly cooked fish. Don't miss their little apple and flambéed Calvados tart, and enjoy good Côtes de Provence house wines. No minimum charge; a meal could cost as little as £5 and as much as £30 a head.

Monsieur Thompson's, *see* page 79.

Le Renoir, 79 Charing Cross Road, WC2 (734–2515). This is a set-menu French restaurant (rare in London), where you can eat adequate French food (the plainer dishes are the most successful) for £6 and £9 (greater choice) for two courses. As it stays open until 2 A.M. this is a useful place to know about; it is also handy for coffee and gateaux. Open at 11:30 A.M.

Rouxl Britannia, Triton Court, 14 Finsbury Square, EC2 (256–6997) and 4 Sydney Street, SW3 (352–3433). This country's top restaurateurs, Michel and Albert Roux, serve a French and English menu at their two *sous vide* (boil in the bag) restaurants. Gourmet meals are prepared elsewhere to excellent standards, sealed and assembled at these two chic restaurants. You could say that the method raises TV dinners to an art form.

St. Quentin, *see* page 73.

La Tante Claire, *see* page 83.

Thierry's, 342 King's Road, SW3 (352–3365). Long a Chelsea favorite, the atmosphere is intimate, with dim lights, prints on the walls, and lots of plants. Standard French cooking with a touch of flair can be chosen from a menu that changes weekly. Typical offerings might be mussels in white wine soup, clams stuffed with herbs, duck pate, and any variety of meats, poultry, and fish accompanied by well-prepared vegetables. To top it off, a souffle or creme brulee. Main courses average £6; a complete meal for two will be about £30. One of the best, and best value, three course lunches for £6.50.

GREEK

Kalamaras, 76–78 Inverness Mews, W2 (727–9122). Kalamaras serves the kind of Greek food you hope to eat in a restaurant in Greece and seldom do. Stelios Platonas imports his own herbs, and recreates authentic and long-forgotten dishes. The decor is very atmospheric, especially when the music adds its distinctive voice, and the wine list offers some of the best Greek wines available in London. Meals are long-drawn out affairs here. Expect to spend £15–£20 per person. There is a branch practically next door, at No. 66, but without a liquor license.

Rodos, 59 St. Giles High Street, WC2 (836–3177).

One of the most authentic of London's many kebab houses. The kitchen is part of the dining room and the menu is classic stuff: *kebabs, moussaka, dolmades,* lamb casseroles, red mullet and garlicky prawns, honey-drenched pistachio-studded pastries, Turkish Delight and pungent Greek coffee. A popular meal is the *mezedakia*—a succession of appetisers and samples of all the main dishes for an all-in £10. A meal for two with Retsina and coffee averages £30.

INDIAN/PAKISTANI

Bombay Brasserie, Courtfield Close, SW7 (370–4040). An enormous elegant room decorated Raj style in the unlikely setting of the rather staid Kensington hotel Bailey's. Nonetheless, the Brasserie attracts a fashionable clientele who don't mind paying prices that are rather more than Londoners associate with Indian food. The £7.95 buffet lunch is an excellent value; for dinner expect to spend £30 for two.

    Last Days of the Raj, 42 Dean Street, W1 (439–0972). By far the most elegant, spacious and comfortable of the smart new Indian restaurants popping up around London. The food is distinctive, lightly spiced and quite delicious. The set meal is a perfect introduction, but choosing from the helpful à la carte menu we would recommend king *prawn massala, prawn puree, tahka dal* (lentils cooked with herbs and spices). A party of between four and six could try the whole leg of baby lamb which is served garnished with pistachio and nuts, costs £30, and requires 24 hours' notice. A multi-course meal for two including Indian lager will average £30.

    The Standard Indian, *see* page 71.

INTERNATIONAL

Blakes, 33 Roland Gardens, SW7 (370–6701). In the basement below Blake's Hotel is this slickly run restaurant, where a media clientele relax in an almost film-set decor—stunning flower arrangements, Thai suits of armor in glass cases, plenty of black and chrome, and all picked out by spotlights. The menu is truly international, and carries both Szechuan duck with roasted salt and pepper, and Italian bresaola. A three-course meal here, including a moderately priced wine from the French wine list, will cost £45 for two.

Le Caprice, *see* page 56.

The Neal Street Restaurant, 26 Neal Street, WC2 (836–8368). This elegant restaurant hung with fine contemporary art is part of the Conran empire. There is an essentially Italian menu but also dishes such as roasted quail with sweet and sour onions. Menu changes with the season; from £20 a head.

Pomegranates, 94 Grosvenor Road, SW1 (828–6560). A basement restaurant with reception area, private dining rooms, and dim lighting. The Chinese chef recreates varied dishes: giant grilled shrimp with creole sauce, piquant Welsh salt duck with white onion sauce. The owner used to be in the wine trade and chooses the wine list. Lunch and dinner; from £15 a head.

ITALIAN

Bertorelli's, *see* page 34.

Cafe Italien, 19–23 Charlotte Street, W1 (636–4174). Bertorelli's has gone, and in its place is Cafe Italien. There's a Bertorelli Room at the rear for old time's sake (same menu), but the rest of the vast premises has been gutted and relaunched as a wine bar and Italian cafe. Open for lunch, tea, and dinner. From £5 a head.

Luigi's, 15 Tavistock Street, WC2 (240–1795). This

Covent Garden restaurant, predating the current fashionable boom, is a friendly place with two small rooms—the upstairs one being the quieter—and a heavy theater slant to its decor and clientele. An extensive menu of all the usual Italian dishes, plus seasonal specialties such as pheasant, partridge, and lobster. Also a good range of liquored coffees. About £35 for two.

Meridiana, 169 Fulham Road, SW3 (589–8815). Also popular among the show biz fraternity, Meridiana is in an elegant, cool white building at the fashionable Chelsea end of Fulham Road. An open-air terrace for summer dining is the perfect spot for excellent pasta, chicken, veal, and seafood. £35 for two.

JAPANESE

Ajimura, *see* page 35.

Masako, 6–8 St. Christopher's Place, W1 (935–1579). One of London's first Japanese restaurants and always reliable for traditional food in authentic surroundings offset by the smart shops between Wigmore and Oxford Streets. Apart from sukiyaki, terriyaki, and sashimi, try yosenabe—assorted seafood and vegetables in a hot broth; or kushiyaki—skewered meat, seafood, and vegetables grilled with sauce and served on a sizzling hot iron plate. From £15 a head.

KOREAN

Arirang, 31/32 Poland Street, W1 (437–6633). Korean food is just beginning to catch on in London, and this was one of the first on the scene. The somewhat garish, grotto-like room has friendly waitresses to help you through the menu. You can try pickled cabbage that sears the mouth, but complements delicious raw beef. Most other dishes are cooked at your table. Dessert? Delicately sculpted fresh fruit. £20 for two.

MEXICAN

Cafe Pacifico, 5 Langley Street, WC2 (379–7728). Yet another former Covent Garden warehouse which, since its conversion, is bustling, noisy, and fun, often patronized by dancers and exercisers from nearby studios. Here you can get well-mixed cocktails and the usual nachos, tacos, and enchiladas, as well as some more unusual items. Not terribly authentic, but at £20 for two, no one complains.

SEAFOOD

La Croisette, 168 Ifield Road, SW10 (373–3694) and **Le Suquet,** 104 Draycott Avenue, SW3 (581–1785). Two delightful South of France restaurants famous for their stunning *plateau de fruits de mer.* Also delicious are French and English oysters, superb fish, lightly cooked and served with simple, tasty sauces. £20 should cover a meal at La Croisette; the average cost of a three-course meal at Le Suquet is £5 higher.

    Geales, *see* page 78.

    The Seashell, 33–35 Lisson Grove, NW1 (723–8703). Considered the best "fish and chippie" in London. There's always a line for fish, which is cooked to order. Takeaway or dine here—bring your own wine. Closed Sunday and Monday. Around £5 a head.

    Sheekeys, *see* page 44.

THAI

Bhan Thai, 35 Marloes Road, W8 (937–9960). Seek out this cozy basement restaurant in Kensington for delicious, spicy Siamese cooking in a friendly ambience. Start with *dim sum* dumplings with plum sauce, sate sticks, and spring rolls. Fried fish in chili and spices is a must, and there are many outstanding pork and chicken dishes made with a variety of authentic spices. An out-of-the-ordinary meal in relaxed surroundings at £30 for two. Also at 21a Frith Street, W1 (437–8504).

VEGETARIAN

Compton Green, *see* page 47.

Cranks, 8 Marshall Street, W1 (437–9431). Cranks pioneered vegetarian food in London in the days when it was thought cranky to eat nut cutlets and the like. Try wholemeal pancakes with various vegetables and cheese or Brazil and cashew nut roast with chestnut and tomato stuffing. Main dishes average £3.25.

Food for Thought, 31 Neal Street, WC2 (836–0239). The customers spill out on the sidewalk at this incredibly popular Covent Garden establishment, which has cramped tables in the basement. The place is very popular with budget- and health-concious kids who are after quiches and salads and stir-fried vegetables with brown rice. £4 per person; no reservations. Useful carry-out service.

Pubs and Wine Bars

The pub, or public house, evolved out of the Roman inn—a place to get a drink, a meal, and a bed for the night. The pub differs in that it doesn't provide accommodations, but it is supposed to provide a welcoming atmosphere, a wide range of drinks, and maybe food and entertainment.

People tend to stand up in pubs, in groups or leaning on the bar, although some tables and chairs are usually available. The most popular drink by far is draught beer, which will taste flat and tepid to an American, or lager, a light beer served chilled, which is more like bottled American beer.

For some time now, many English have eschewed mass-produced commercial beers for "real ale" from small breweries that use traditional beer-making methods. These are much stronger and more potent than the big brand name beers, and are also an acquired taste.

Membership of the European Community has lowered taxes on imported wine and has slowly changed the drinking habits of many English people. Wine bars are very popular; here there are usually more tables and chairs, a wider selection of food, and, of course, wine to drink—often with a number of vintage bottles available by the glass.

A third drinking change in London of late has been the resurgence of interest in cocktails. Some pubs and wine bars are being revamped as 1930s-style cocktail bars with a range of new concoctions as well as the traditional mixes.

London has several thousand pubs and wine bars— indeed, a bewildering variety—but you will generally receive a friendly welcome from the bar staff and locals, particularly if you show an interest in the types of beers or wines available.

Unfortunately, while London's pubs are excellent places to sit and relax, you can't just walk in at any time. The U.K.'s strict licensing laws determine pub operating hours and when drinks may be served in restaurants. Most pubs have licenses that require them to open from 11 A.M. to 3 P.M., and again from 5:30 to 11 P.M., Monday through Saturday. On Sundays they open from noon to 2 P.M. and 7 to 10:30 P.M. Restaurants may usually serve alcohol later, but you must order food with it. Patrons also know to pay cold cash upon being served—you don't run a tab in a pub as you would in an American bar.

Here, then, is a necessarily brief selection of pubs, wine bars, and cocktail bars.

The Red Lion, Waverton Street, W1 (499-1307). Not far from the Hilton Hotel in a quiet Mayfair backwater, this was once an 18th-century farmhouse. It has a pleasant terrace with rustic furniture for outdoor drinking on warm summer evenings. Genteel bars and an attractive restaurant.

The Running Footman, 5 Charles Street, W1 (499-8239). Another famous Mayfair pub with a long history. The name derives from the footmen who used to run before a carriage to clear the way and pay tolls. Serves real ale.

The Grenadier, 18 Wilton Row, Belgrave Square, SW1 (235-3074). In the heart of "Upstairs, Downstairs" land, this 1812 pub, built as the Duke of Wellington's officers' mess, is said to be haunted by the ghost of an officer flogged to death for cheating at cards. King George IV was a patron. It has a candlelit restaurant.

St. Stephen's Tavern, 10 Bridge Street, SW1 (930-3230). Rub shoulders with Members of Parliament in this "local" opposite the Houses of Parliament. It has a "division bell" that rings to summon MPs back to the House to vote. Restaurant walls are lined with cartoons of past MP customers.

The Sherlock Holmes, 10 Northumberland Street, WC2 (930-2644). Named after the fictional detective created by Arthur Conan Doyle, who was a regular customer. Contains a tiny room that is a replica of Holmes' study at 221b Baker Street. Restaurant.

The Anchor, 1 Bankside, SE1 (407-1577). Situated in the Southwark district on the south side of the Thames, this famous riverside pub was rebuilt after being destroyed in the Great Fire of 1666. It is said that Dr. Johnson worked on his dictionary here; nearby was Shakespeare's Globe Theatre.

The Angel, 101 Bermondsey Wall East, SE16 (237-3608). Worth making the trip to this riverside pub for the views of Tower Bridge from its balcony overlooking the Thames. Captain Cook drank here when he wasn't discovering bits of Australia and New Zealand—including Botany Bay, which he named—in the 18th century.

The Clarence, 53 Whitehall, SW1 (930-4808). A Dickensian period pub with wandering minstrels performing Monday through Thursday.

Queens Arms, 94 Draycott Avenue, SW3 (589-0570). A typical "local" in Chelsea. You can join in the singing to live music on Saturday. An excellent place to get the real feel of a British pub.

The Frog and Firkin, 41 Tavistock Crescent, W11 (727-9250). A firkin is an olde English measure of liquid —but apart from the name, the Frog and Firkin is worth visiting for real ale and its traditional pub pianist most lunchtimes and evenings.

Brahms & Liszt, 19 Russell Street, WC2 (240-3661). The name is cockney rhyming slang for drunk. This is a lively, noisy Covent Garden wine bar with a good selection of wines and food.

Cork & Bottle, 44-46 Cranbourn Street, WC2 (734-

6592). A basement with cozy alcoves, the Cork & Bottle is one of London's oldest wine bars. There's a fine selection of pates and cheeses, as well as a few hot dishes—and a wide range of good-value wines.

El Vino, 47 Fleet Street, EC4 (353-6786). Rub shoulders with Fleet Street's editors and hacks and the Law Courts' barristers and lawyers in this historic bar. Gentlemen must wear jacket and tie, while ladies are expected to sit at the tables—not stand at the bar. Not a place for a feminist!

Jules Bar, 85 Jermyn Street, London W1 (930-4700). Popular cocktail bar on one of London's smartest streets. Red plush upholstery and a pianist.

Penny's Place, 6 King Street, WC2 (836-4553). A fruit-and-vegetable era Covent Garden pub converted to a wine bar. Two narrow rooms upstairs and down, with bistro food in both. Friendly and popular.

Peppermint Park, 13 Upper St. Martin's Lane, WC2 (836-5234). One of London's new-generation cocktail bars with restaurant. A riot of green and pink decor and loud, taped music. Extensive drinks list and bar food.

Rumours, 33 Wellington Street, WC2 (836-0038). Very popular Covent Garden bar in a converted warehouse. Big and spacious, but usually crowded. Voted cocktail bar of the year in a newspaper poll.

Nightlife

Be it the noise and sweat of a packed disco or a rock club, the intimacy of a cabaret or a small dance floor, or some cool jazz to help unwind after an exhausting day of sightseeing, London can meet your nightlife needs. Those places serving alcohol are licensed to operate at certain hours. The rules are mind-boggling, and the exceptions even more confusing; suffice it to know that most places find a way around the rules and will do their utmost to help quench any thirst that may arise.

The Hippodrome, Charing Cross Road (437-4311), in the heart of the West End, should be top priority for any disco fan. Formerly the legendary Talk of the Town nightclub, it takes its name from the original theater that occupied the site and is, quite simply, the most stunning disco in London.

Superb sound and lighting systems, loud music as up-to-date as you can get, a hydraulically-operated dance floor, music video, live entertainment, and some of London's most colorful characters all vie for your attention here. Style is vital if you want to get in. There's an à la carte restaurant. Admission is £6–10, depending on the night and the entertainment. Closed Sunday.

Stringfellow's, Upper St. Martin's Lane (240-5534), across the street, is a film- and show-business haunt sharing the same owner as the Hippodrome. It, too, boasts excellent lighting and sound, and is open until the early hours of the morning. Food and drink are expensive; be sure to dress smart and chichi. Admission £6–12.50. Closed Sunday.

For live music, the **Limelight,** at 136 Shaftesbury Avenue, stays open until 3:30 A.M. Further north, London's newest venue, the **Town and Country Club,** has opened at 9–17 Highgate Road, NW5. Although slightly inconvenient—take the tube to Kentish Town—this is the place that's attracting the names from both sides of the Atlantic. Admission charge depends on who's performing.

Samantha's, 3 New Burlington St., W1 (734-6249). A long-established disco with plenty of atmosphere. Open Monday to Saturday, 9–3:30; admission varies with time of night and whether you are a member—but they observe a strict dress code. Admission charge £4–£6; annual membership£60.

The Camden Palace, Camden High Street (387-0428) just north of Euston Station, is noted for brash, colorful "creatures of the night" who frequent it, and for some of the best music in town. Live acts are featured regularly—often of an eccentric nature—but no one can visit the Camden Palace and fail to be entertained. Admission £3–5. Closed Sunday and Monday.

Ronnie Scott's, 47 Frith Street (439-0747), off Shaftesbury Avenue, is known to jazz fans around the world. It is the London home to Ella Fitzgerald, Sonny Rollins, Roland Kirk, Nina Simone, and dozens of others. The atmosphere is intimate and relaxed, the food and drink basic but reasonable, and the entertainment rarely less than first rate. Admission £7–8. Closed Sunday.

Pizza Express, 10 Dean Street (439-8722), presents lesser-known jazz artists. Food and drink are relatively inexpensive. Admission varies; usually £6–10.

The Donmar Warehouse, 41 Earlham Street (379-6565), is one of Covent Garden's nightlife outposts. There's a late-late show, and the acts are always entertaining. Mainstream rock clubs are topped by **The Mar-**

quee, 90 Wardour Street (437-6603), a legendary club that is small, always crowded, and only for those with great stamina.

For pop, rock, and jazz, also check *Time Out* and the London *Standard* for concerts at Hammersmith Odeon, Dominion, Earl's Court, and Wembley.

Note: London has more than its share of traditional nightclubs full of tired businessmen and hostesses. The luxury hotels also have their rooms for dining and dancing, and there are numerous restaurants with pocket handkerchief dance floors. In our experience, you rarely get the best food or entertainment at these establishments.

Index

FODOR'S TRAVEL GUIDES

Here is a complete list of Fodor's Travel Guides, available in current editions; most are also available in a British edition published by Hodder & Stoughton.

U.S. GUIDES

Alaska
American Cities (Great Travel Values)
Arizona including the Grand Canyon
Atlantic City & the New Jersey Shore
Boston
California
Cape Cod & the Islands of Martha's Vineyard & Nantucket
Carolinas & the Georgia Coast
Chesapeake
Chicago
Colorado
Dallas/Fort Worth
Disney World & the Orlando Area (Fun in)
Far West
Florida
Forth Worth (see Dallas)
Galveston (see Houston)
Georgia (see Carolinas)
Grand Canyon (see Arizona)
Greater Miami & the Gold Coast
Hawaii
Hawaii (Great Travel Values)
Houston & Galveston
I-10: California to Florida
I-55: Chicago to New Orleans
I-75: Michigan to Florida
I-80: San Francisco to New York
I-95: Maine to Miami
Jamestown (see Williamsburg)
Las Vegas including Reno & Lake Tahoe (Fun in)
Los Angeles & Nearby Attractions
Martha's Vineyard (see Cape Cod)
Maui (Fun in)
Nantucket (see Cape Cod)
New England
New Jersey (see Atlantic City)
New Mexico
New Orleans
New Orleans (Fun in)
New York City
New York City (Fun in)
New York State
Orlando (see Disney World)
Pacific North Coast
Philadelphia
Reno (see Las Vegas)
Rockies
San Diego & Nearby Attractions
San Francisco (Fun in)
San Francisco plus Marin County & the Wine Country
The South
Texas
U.S.A.
Virgin Islands (U.S. & British)

Virginia
Waikiki (Fun in)
Washington, D.C.
Williamsburg, Jamestown & Yorktown

FOREIGN GUIDES

Acapulco (see Mexico City)
Acapulco (Fun in)
Amsterdam
Australia, New Zealand & the South Pacific
Austria
The Bahamas
The Bahamas (Fun in)
Barbados (Fun in)
Beijing, Guangzhou & Shanghai
Belgium & Luxembourg
Bermuda
Brazil
Britain (Great Travel Values)
Canada
Canada (Great Travel Values)
Canada's Maritime Provinces plus Newfoundland & Labrador
Cancún, Cozumel, Mérida & the Yucatán
Caribbean
Caribbean (Great Travel Values)
Central America
Copenhagen (see Stockholm)
Cozumel (see Cancún)
Eastern Europe
Egypt
Europe
Europe (Budget)
France
France (Great Travel Values)
Germany: East & West
Germany (Great Travel Values)
Great Britain
Greece
Guangzhou (see Beijing)
Helsinki (see Stockholm)
Holland
Hong Kong & Macau
Hungary
India, Nepal & Sri Lanka
Ireland
Israel
Italy
Italy (Great Travel Values)
Jamaica (Fun in)
Japan
Japan (Great Travel Values)
Jordan & the Holy Land
Kenya
Korea
Labrador (see Canada's Maritime Provinces)
Lisbon
Loire Valley
London

London (Fun in)
London (Great Travel Values)
Luxembourg (see Belgium)
Macau (see Hong Kong)
Madrid
Mazatlan (see Mexico's Baja)
Mexico
Mexico (Great Travel Values)
Mexico City & Acapulco
Mexico's Baja & Puerto Vallarta, Mazatlan, Manzanillo, Copper Canyon
Montreal (Fun in)
Munich
Nepal (see India)
New Zealand
Newfoundland (see Canada's Maritime Provinces)
1936 . . . on the Continent
North Africa
Oslo (see Stockholm)
Paris
Paris (Fun in)
People's Republic of China
Portugal
Province of Quebec
Puerto Vallarta (see Mexico's Baja)
Reykjavik (see Stockholm)
Rio (Fun in)
The Riviera (Fun on)
Rome
St. Martin/St. Maarten (Fun in)
Scandinavia
Scotland
Shanghai (see Beijing)
Singapore
South America
South Pacific
Southeast Asia
Soviet Union
Spain
Spain (Great Travel Values)
Sri Lanka (see India)
Stockholm, Copenhagen, Oslo, Helsinki & Reykjavik
Sweden
Switzerland
Sydney
Tokyo
Toronto
Turkey
Vienna
Yucatán (see Cancún)
Yugoslavia

SPECIAL-INTEREST GUIDES

Bed & Breakfast Guide: North America
Royalty Watching
Selected Hotels of Europe
Selected Resorts and Hotels of the U.S.
Ski Resorts of North America
Views to Dine by around the World

AVAILABLE AT YOUR LOCAL BOOKSTORE OR WRITE TO FODOR'S TRAVEL PUBLICATIONS, INC., 201 EAST 50th STREET, NEW YORK, NY 10022.